THE AL QAEDA DISCOURSE OF THE GREATER KUFR

THE AL QAEDA DISCOURSE OF THE GREATER KUFR

Daurius Figueira

iUniverse, Inc.
New York Lincoln Shanghai

The Al Qaeda Discourse of the Greater Kufr

iUniverse, Inc.

For information address:
iUniverse, Inc.
2021 Pine Lake Road, Suite 100
Lincoln, NE 68512
www.iuniverse.com

ISBN: 0-595-33613-2

Printed in the United States of America

TO MY BROTHERS IN THE STRUGGLE SURENDRANATH CAPILDEO AND NICHOLAS FLEMMING.

I was raised in the Roman Catholic Church baptized at birth; I made my first communion and was confirmed. At age 17 I became a born again Christian of the Churches of Christ. For some five years I studied the New Testament to the extent of becoming familiar with the language of the New Testament, koine Greek. After five years of intense study problems of faith in a God that suffers with a blood lust and became flesh to satisfy this blood lust arose. I was then drawn to the virulent monotheism of Islam and the uncompromising discourse of Tawhid. Before I decided to walk the path of Islam I mouthed publicly that my return to a praxis of surrender to the All Knowing would only be premised upon being Muslim. I am now centered in Islam only because of its relevance to me at the level of the idea. I came to Islam seeking no social prominence, no material possessions, no relief from physical infirmities all I seek within Islam is liberation at the level of the idea all the rest is the purview of Allah (swt). In the time I have been a Muslim I have experienced the reality that the most pervasive and potent enemies of Islam are those that call themselves Muslims. Whilst we rant and rave about the kuffir and kufr the munafikun of the Ummah strive diligently to destroy the Ummah from inside out. The fifth columnists of Islam are of the shaitan.

In the name of Allah, the beneficent, the merciful.

162. Say: Surely my prayer and my sacrifice and my life and my death are (all) for Allah, the Lord of the worlds;

163. No associate has He; and this am I commanded, and I am the first of those who submit.

Say: What! Shall I seek a lord other than Allah? And he is the Lord of all things; and no soul earns (evil) but against itself, and no bearer of burden shall bear the burden of another, then to your Lord is your return, so He will inform you of that in which you differed.

The Holy Quran
Surah: The Cattle

Contents

Acknowledgments

I wish to thank my wife and son, and all other persons who have in any way contributed to this work. To my sisters and brothers of the Ummah who fight the dajjal that is Al Qaeda, All Praises are only for Allah (swt).

Daurius Figueira.

Chapter 1

ISLAMIC DISCOURSE: GENERALITIES

It is with reluctance and trepidation the researcher now begins the process of creating the textual existence of his journey of discovery and research through the fields of experience summed up in this text as the Islamic discourse. From the outset the researcher was always mindful of the impossibility of the task of seeking to embrace the sum total of all perceptions that flow within the parameters of Islamic discourse. The researcher was therefore evading the Orientalist enterprise of creating essentialist matrices, which trapped the "essences" of the Islamic worldview thereby giving birth to the phenomenon aptly termed "homo Islamicus" (Legacy of Islam). The researcher "saw" diversity within parameters but the shock of discovery was in the varieties of diversity that spoke to the researcher.

But one must now answer one question before one goes about building the text of diversity. That is; what are the parameters? The researcher found a simple answer to the question of limits, to the boundaries that separate Islam from the "other/s." The answers came from the persons who carry and animate the discourse and the simplicity of the answer in itself offered insights into the ontological structure of the Islamic discourse. The space that encompasses the Islamic condition is summed up by the five pillars of Islam. These are:

(a) The testimonial of Islam, which is "There is no divinity but the Divine and Mohammed is his Prophet."
(b) Salat or prayer five times daily at minimum.
(c) Fasting especially during the month of Ramadan.
(d) Zakat
(e) Hajj or pilgrimage to Mecca.

But even in this attempt to define Islamic space there is diversity for in the five pillars enumerated the only practice which approaches "orthodoxy" in some form is the acceptance of the concept of unity of the Godhead or tawhid. The testimonial of the unity and singularity of the Godhead or Shahadah and the prophethood of Muhammad is then the only attempt within the discourse to define access to its space. But no definite and rigid orthodoxy of access has ever been developed within the discourse which has enabled the creation of a powered elite who embraced or excluded perceptions hence persons through their dominant discursive structures of "orthodoxy."

The raging debate within the Islamic discourse has throughout the centuries, remained just that a raging debate, over the perceptions and actions that constitute orthodoxy. Islamic discourse has never had to cope with the discursive cannibalism that plagued Western Christianity contributing to its hegemonic decline and defeat. The fundamental reason why the Islamic discourse continues to exert its energies on debate over "essences" and "conditions" of an Islamic existence lies in the fact that there is no mediator between Allah and human in the Islamic discourse.

The Islamic discourse is therefore not carried, defined or "othodoxized" by a priestly caste. The discourse is defined only through revelation of Allah to humanity via the prophet Muhammad (uwbp). Revelation was made via language and is transmitted throughout time through the written word contained in the Qur'an. The text exists, the giver of revelation and the final arbitrator in any dispute over the discursive structures of Islamic discourse. But without the creation of an empowered priestly caste whose duty it was to interpret the text thereby mediating the contact between Allah and humanity, interpretation was left up to the persons who carried no enabling ability to enforce adherence given their consecration into an empowered elite.

Without the ability to mediate, to define, to deny or foster the relationship between Muslim and Allah, the interpreters of the Qur'an in Islam became what they are today learned people whose interpretations are simply that interpretations to be either accepted or rejected by the body of believers, the Ummah. The continued debate over the constitution of orthodoxy in the Islamic discourse is but one instance of a wider field of knowledge, which has enabled the discourse to retain its vitality in the face of relentless, discursive contradictions since the first century AH of its existence. The discursive structures of Islamic discourse enable the discourse to replicate itself across human history in hegemonic dominance or as a resilient minority discourse through the enabling of the formation of, and circulation of various perceptive matrices within the discourse and the resultant circulation of elites.

The specific discursive structures of the Islamic discourse do not resolve contradictions within the discourse by resorting to internecine warfare as the final resolution of contradictions. Discursive contradictions are primarily expressed via language and resolved via the contentions of ideas locked in struggle for hegemony within a discursive field of knowledge. The primary question remains WHY? The researcher can in reply posit the following;

(a) Islamic discourse is to date unable to generate the creation of orthodoxy of ideas. The discourse stresses primarily on an ortho-praxis rather than an ortho-perception. Today debate still rages on the question of the means to discern Muslims from non-Muslims through the application of the five pillars of Islam to the praxis of the individual. The lesson of relevance to the researcher from the discursive positions locked in struggle in this debate is the absence of an orthodoxy in Islamic discourse and more importantly the absence of a priestly caste to mediate the debates.

(b) The rejection of mediation between Allah and mankind has various implications for the discourse. Some of these are the inability to embrace Christ and Christianity and the priesthood. Moreso the laying of responsibility on each believer so motivated to create discursive positions on issues up for debate within the discourse ensures the creation of ideas and ideational contention within the discourse. The path towards the creation of ideational contention and resolution resulting in the circulation of ideational elites within the discourse is not stymied, deflected, or simply closed by the development of a professional class of priests who are empowered by a unique relationship to their god. A discourse without a ruling definition of orthodoxy and an entrenched elite who defines, replicates and polices the orthodoxy is ultimately a discourse, which ceaselessly strives to replicate itself via an ideational mode of production.

Islamic discourse throughout its history as a result is not burdened with the discursive cannibalism of Christianity. Internecine conflict within the discourse is then ultimately linked to struggles for power within the states thrown up by the spaces inhabited by the Ummah and the power relations of and amongst the Ummah. The equation is deliberately stated as above for the discourse embraces neither nationalism nor nation states in its modernist Western formulations nor the hegemony of aggregations, which strive for hegemony over the Ummah. The discourse has therefore fed the creation and contention of anti-monarchist ideas, in the era of the hegemony of monarchists, the creation and contention of ideas against atheist socialism in the era of chic socialism, the creation and contention of ideas against Western style democracy.

Ultimately the creation and contention of ideas against Western modernism and secularisation. The ability to formulate ideas to contend with developments in the discursive fields of attrition and contradiction since its inception shows the versatility of Islamic discourse. Again the question is WHY? The question before as this one are merely rhetorical as the researcher formulates his text within the perceptual fields of Orientalism as an indicator of the Orientalist worldview we of the periphery carry around within the perceptual frameworks through which we perceive the world. From here on the Orientalist exercise ceases, no questions are to be asked, no causalities sought, no matrices erected to constitute the post-modern homo Islamicus.

The question of why no orthodoxy within Islamic discourse is constituted by the Orientalist worldview that an ontology that is God driven is inherently irrational for the existence of God cannot be empirically verified. God driven ontologies can only then follow given irrational paths, which ensure the erosion and defeat of its hegemony by rationalist driven ontologies. The question then of why no orthodoxy in Islamic discourse is but another variant theme constituted by Orientalist discourse.

Even though the researcher sets out to show the uniqueness and versatility of Islamic discourse by constituting a question out of the Orientalist worldview, knowledge is generated by the very same matrices of the worldview that constituted the question to generate and replicate the question and the worldview that constituted it.

The lesson is then very simple you cannot create alternate fields of knowledge in contradiction with and locked in a battle for hegemony with western discourse utilising the discursive structures of the worldview you are seeking to displace, to "de-hegemonize." The text that was created in response to the question "why no orthodoxy in Islamic discourse?" is a text of compromise, a text of discursive "mulattodom," a textual zebra which carries within its structures the seeds of its own defeat when locked in battle with western discourse. Even moreso the text that was constituted by the question "why the versatility of Islamic discourse?"

This is the most despicable question that jumped out of the Orientalist perceptions of the researcher. Again, simply another example of the need to prove to the west, to the white man, that we of the periphery can produce concrete perceptions, perceptive structures, discourses worthy of their worldview, worthy of their notice, worthy of their fear and trepidation. Again the question sprang out of Ontological orientalism in reverse. For we are seeking weapons against the white man's hegemony through constituting discursive weaponry forged in the crucible of his design and technological know-how.

Islamic discourse is then the researchers hegemonic weapon for it is versatile, it responds to a variety of challenges throughout its history failing to recognize that you cannot answer the white man's racism by constituting weapons forged by our self-hatred and self-immolation. The questions are now irrelevant, the text constituted by the questions retained as a reminder to the mental workers of the periphery as is the researcher of the subtle ways in which the racist worldview of the West continues to cloud, to blinker our efforts to perceptually leap out, of dependence, self hatred, self-immolation and oppression. For here on the paramountcy of perceptions is recognized and therein the inability of the researcher to embrace all perceptions that fall within the space delimited by the Islamic discourse.

But moreso the impossibility of the researcher to find, to locate, to fix every perception in its spatial specificity within the spaces of the Islamic discourse and from this exercise in Sisyphean futility to sift, to trap, to produce causalities, explanations, means of rejection of the nexus behind western epistemologies. The researcher defines his enterprise simply then to give voice to the perceptions, by trapping perceptions within a text, we then finalise the exercise in mapping the co-ordinates of discourses. Nothing more, nothing less, the enterprise's mission statement is then to textualize the spoken word, to trap it within texts which are in itself part of the mapping co-ordinates of the enterprise.

The researcher's modus operandi would now be to present the ontology of the Islamic discourse as formulated by the perceptions and experiences of a Muslim.

This ontology is textualized, as a co-ordinate in the mapping exercise for other ontologies would be added to the text as the enterprise proceeds enabling the researcher to plot a map of perceptions. The ontology that follows is the work of Seyyed Hosein Nasr in the texts "Islamic Life and Thought" and "Sufi Essays."

Nasr's ontology was chosen for he identifies himself with the esoteric Sufi perceptions and the resulting worldview. As other ontologies are added to the texts that follow, the enterprise would be afforded the ability to view the diversity of perceptions that flow and combine in the Islamic discourse. Nasr states in "Islamic Life and Thought":

> "Islam is at once a religion and a civilization and social order based upon the revealed principles of the religion. It is an archetypal reality residing eternally in the Divine Intellect and an unfolding of this reality in history and in lives of numerous generations of men from different races and ethnic groups and different localities spreading over most of the surface of the earth."
>
> (Nasr 1981 Page 5)

Again Nasr states:

> "Religion may be considered ultimately as the Divine Guide by the help of which man can overcome the ontological barrier separating him from his divine origin, although in essence he has never been separated from it."
>
> (Nasr 1981 Page 8)

We are therefore in Nasr's ontology to come to grips with his concepts of "the archetypal reality", "the Divine intellect", and the "ontological barrier." At the outset he dismisses what he terms "Cartesian dualism" and its influence upon the western concept of man as being constituted of body and mind. He posits that in keeping with traditional Hermetic and Sapiental worldviews that man transcends dualities for he is constituted by spirit, soul and body. The relevance of the entire enterprise of Nasr is his soul's journey towards unification with the Divine Intellect therefore the paths of re-unification. His ontology is one entirely concerned with freedom through realization of the Truth (al haqq). How does he conceptualise of the entire enterprise of realization?

Nasr conceives of the ontology of liberation in the dance of dualities. These are:

(a) The dance of inward and outward, the duality of esoteric and exoteric meanings and practises, such as the esoteric meaning of Salat, Jihad and the exoteric meaning of the same.
(b) Dance of the Absolute (Mutlaq) and the relative (Muqayyad). The Divine Intellect and the representation of the Divine Intellect; man.
(c) The Uncreated Truth (al-haqq) and the created order (al-khalq).

Nasr states that the Absolute is manifested in the relative in the form of Symbols (rumuz). This manifestation of rumuz is the basis of revelation and makes revelation possible and a reality. Rumuz is therefore an aspect of the ontological reality of things. Man is the image of the Absolute in the relative therefore man is empowered to undertake the path of becoming which culminates in Being. Rumuz (symbols) is the basis, the foundation of the hierarchic structure of the relative universe and enables the existence of the multiple states of being that is Man. All things are theophanies of the Divine Names and Qualities and derive their existence from the One Being who alone is; therefore there is Transcendent Unity of Being/Wahdat al-Wujud. And the Universal or Perfect Man/Al-Inasn Al Kamil. Tawhid/Unity is manifested in the Nature of Reality, which is the Oneness of the Divine Essence, which is and is nothingness.

The theophany of the Divine Essence through the Divine Name and Qualities and man is the total theophany/tagalli of the Names and Qualities of the Divine Essence. The duality of man as the theophany of the Divine Names and Qualities and the theophany of the Divine Essence through the Divine Name and Qualities enables the determination of different states of being in man. What then is this journey upon the paths or Way/Tariqah to God? Nasr states that the tariqah to the Divine Essence is one based on the attainment of spiritual states, which are in themselves virtues/Mahasin or fada'il. The virtue attained is a state of being having a definite ontological aspect. How has Nasr's worldview influenced his perceptions, instances of this would now be presented via his text.

On Islam and secularism he states:

> "We see, therefore, that in nearly every domain of life the unitary principles of Islam are challenged by secular ideas and the Islamic world is faced with the mortal danger of "polytheism or shirk," that is the setting up of various modern European ideas as gods alongside Allah."

> "When the illusion of the separation between the soul and the Divine Self is removed we realise that there is but one principle dominant in every mode of manifestation, and that the reality we saw in secularism as a competing principle with religion has been no more than the realities of fantasies of a soul not yet awakened from the dream of negligence and forgetfulness."

> (Nasr 1981 Page 14)

On Islam and freedom he states:

> "The discussion of the concept of freedom in the West is so deeply influenced by the Renaissance and post-Renaissance notion of man as a being in revolt against Heaven and master of the earth that it is difficult to envisage the very meaning of freedom in the context of a traditional civilization such as that of Islam."

> (Nasr 1981 Page 16)

> "The most crucial test for the actual realization of means to attain freedom in Islam has been the degree to which it has been able to keep alive within its bosom ways of spiritual realization leading to inner freedom."

> (Nasr 1981 Page 16)

On the Shar'iah, Nasr states:

> "Every discussion of Islamic law involves the most basic religious beliefs and attitudes of Muslims. This is because in Islam the Divine

Will manifests itself concretely as specific law, and not abstractly as more or less general moral injunctions."

(Nasr 1981 Page 24)

"Therefore the Shari'ah being an eternal truth belonging to a higher order of existence, is by no means abrogated if it does not conform to the Divine Law."

(Nasr 1981 Page 26)

"Only by accepting the validity of the Shari'ah and especially of the personal laws promulgated by it and by relying on these laws can Islamic society face the problems of the modern world."

(Nasr 1981 Page 30)

On the role of women Nasr states:

"In Islam the role of men and women is seen as complimentary rather than competitive. Before God man and woman stand as equals."

(Nasr 1981 Page 212)

"Hence it may be said that in their relation with the meta-cosmic reality they are equal. But on the cosmic level, which means the psychological, biological and social levels, their roles are complimentary."

(Nasr 1981 Page 212)

"Islam believes that in the social order duties must be divided in such a way that men are able to perform what enables them to realise their potentialities as men, and likewise women must have a role in conformity with the genius and nature of their sex."

(Nasr 1981 Page 212)

"A normal and healthy society, of which the traditional Islamic society is an excellent example, is one in which both men and women are given the possibilities to develop fully their natures and to contribute to that richness and diversity which characterise creation and reflect the Unity of the Divine Principle."

(Nasr 1981 Page 212)

It is then a journey of discovery through Nasr's ontology and textual instances of his worldview expressed as he wrestles with the discursive contradictions with Western capitalist discourse. From the outset it is apparent that his ontology threw up a specific language of explanation, of rationality, of causality that occupies a distinct space in the flow of perceptions that are held together to form Islamic discourse. He speaks, he explains, his causalities, his perceptions, his language are all based upon his specific ontology, his worldview, which he subsumes within the Islamic discourse.

In effect Nasr speaks as an esoteric visionary who straddles an esoteric praxis in his search for immersion in the totality of Being. You are able to touch; to experience the tension in his texts dealing with the esoteric orthopraxis of Islam for this tension is common to all adherents of the esoteric ontology in an Islam dominated by an esoteric ortho praxis. In his quest for the ontological states of virtue in the tariqah/Way to the Divine Essence the ortho praxis can in effect become hindrances in the path of an outer worldly focused ontology.

Nasr therefore states:

> "By and large, the Islamic tradition has provided a vast umbrella under which views as different as those of Rhazes and an Ibn' Arabi have been expressed and taught. If there has been tension, it has usually been between the esoteric and the exoteric dimensions of the tradition but this is a tension which is of a creative nature and lies within the structure of the Islamic tradition itself."

(Nasr 1981 Page 22)

Given his recognition of the tensions that exist both inwardly and outwardly, the salient lesson of the journey through Nasr's texts is his refusal to abandon traditional Islamic esoteric discursive structures in a bid to respond to the perceived potent threat of the modernism and secularisation of western discourse. In fact he deepens his Islamic worldview, his personal convictions as a Muslim by embracing the ontology/worldview of esoteric Islamic discourse. For him on the level of personal psychic pilgrimage the journey to and through Islamic esoterica was the means to ensure, to shore up, to build fortifications, necessary to withstand the relentless attacks of the Western discourse upon his definition of himself as a Muslim.

We leave the texts of Nasr as the journey continues and we now textualize the text titled "The Resurgence of Islam, and our Liberation from the Colonial Yoke" by Maryam Jameelah. At the outset we journey to the text seeking Ms.Jameelah's ontology finding the following:

"The superiority of the West in energy, organization and technology was in large measure responsible for its domination over the rest of the world. The Muslims along with all other non-European peoples everywhere, both primitive and highly civilized, succumbed not so much because of their "decadence" or "stagnation" but rather because Western materialism is a virulent malignant disease capable of destroying even a healthy people. Modern Western materialism could therefore be compared to a cancer which has consumed the earth as cancer in an individual man destroys his body."

(Jameelah 1980 Pages 526-527)

"Modern science and technology is based on pure materialism. Nature is regarded as entirely profane to be manipulated and exploited for profit without any restraint."

(Jameelah 1980 Pages 27-28)

"We must cease to judge our countries and our peoples by the criterion of "development". We must liberate science from the philosophy of materialism, resist its dehumanising effects and unify this fragmented concept of knowledge to begin once again to create a new Islamic science on our own initiative."

(Jameelah 1980 Page 28)

"Finally, we must repudiate the erroneous ideal if material progress and well being as the aim of human life. We should not allow ourselves to be misled by the delusion that poverty, disease, suffering and death can be eliminated nor should we try to do so but instead we must combat social injustice, political tyranny and help the victims as much as possible wherever we find them. It is no coincidence that those societies which have attempted to satisfy all the physical needs of man have only succeeded in creating an inward spiritual poverty, which is a mockery of their external wealth."

(Jameelah 1980 Pages 28-29)

Ms. Jameelah's worldview when applied to the issue of liberation and the post-colonial conditions created instances in the text as follows:

"Along with all other non-European peoples of the world, we fell under foreign colonial domination and are now in the post-colonial period being speedily absorbed into the mainstream of modern Western civilization."

(Jameelah 1980 Page 5)

"None of the Muslim states have been able to solve any of the social, economic, political or cultural conflicts inherited by them from colonialism."

(Jameelah 1980 Page 6)

"Although enormous wealth of oil resources on a scale undreamt of before, have become available to some of the Muslim states of Western Asia, none of these material advantages have been able to arrest and reverse the rapid decay of Islamic civilization, which is continuing today with ever growing speed at the hands of the Muslims themselves."

(Jameelah 1980 Page 6)

"Western ideals and values, or more accurately, the lack of them, are exported to the Muslim world by means of the imported films, radio and television programs, both in English and the native languages..."

(Jameelah 1980 Page 10)

"This cultural invasion via the mass-media is far more effective in destroying our indigenous life-style than previously conducted through their educational systems alone because this affects the illiterate masses of peasants and workers whereas formerly during the colonial period,it reached only a tiny privileged elite."

(Jameelah 1980 Page 10)

"The breakdown of our society thus continues at an ever accelerating pace, producing a new generation of rootless, cynical and alienated people. The results of our abject slavery to the colonial yoke in the post-colonial era can be clearly seen everywhere."

(Jameelah 1980 Page 16)

"Instead of the "white man's burden" and Europe's civilizing mission" to the "benighted East", the colonial yoke is today justified and expanded under the slogan's of "modernization", "development" and "progress"."

(Jameelah 1980 Page 19)

"The inferiority complex which resulted from our subjection to colonial rule, produced an abundant crop of goslings who preached open co-operation with our enemies and the adoption of their culture and materialistic outlook on life, guided by expediency and opportunism..."

(Jameelah 1980 Page 19)

"In our struggle to liberate ourselves from the colonial yoke, we must revive the memories of all our great valiant Mujahideen who struggled against European imperialism."

(Jameelah 1980 Page 23)

"The memories of their heroic deeds must be revived and retold in all the school texts for our children and youth to inspire leadership for the future."

(Jameelah 1980 Page 24)

"If the Islamic Revolution is to achieve success, it is imperative that nationalism and the concept of the national state be repudiated absolutely..."

(Jameelah 1980 Pages 24-25)

"The aim must not be narrow exclusive national sovereignty but Muslim unity and revival of Khilafat. Once Khilafat is established, Islam will once again become in the next century of the Hijra a powerful political and spiritual force in world affairs."

(Jameelah 1980 Page 35)

"A Muslim must fight to defend not only the state and community but also himself whenever necessary. According to the Shari'ah, all Muslim men have the right to be armed. Muslim leaders struggling for the restoration of the Shar'iah must be brought together so they can meet and plan, co-ordinate and unify their Jihad and thus avoid the catastrophic mistake of nationalist battles for "liberation.""

(Jameelah 1980 Page 30)

"We must openly call on all Muslim heads of state to submit to the Shari'ah. Once they have refused, they have admitted the fact to all that they are nothing more than munafiqin (hypocrites) and must be deposed by the Muslim community as the Shah was deposed in Iran."

(Jameelah 1980 Page 30)

Jameelah's worldview is plainly different from that of Nasr's in its emphasis. It is obvious that Jameelah is grounded in an ortho praxis of the exoteric path taken to its furthest development as she openly insists that an Islamic revolution is now needed to ensure the ability of the discourse to not only withstand the attacks of Western discourse but to allow the Islamic discourse to go on the offensive. For her the Islamic revolution is totalistic, as it must address the totality of the post-colonial condition of domination. The Islamic revolution would not only address issues of technological backwardness, or western domination through science and technology, it has to address the psychic legacy of colonialism carried around by post-colonial Muslims. This revolution is to be attained by any means necessary moreso the Iranian Islamic revolution of 1979 is the model for Jameelah's Islamic revolution. Her worldview is again another example of a worldview based on differing emphases drawn from the Islamic discourse flowing and contending within and with the flow of ideas that make up the Islamic discourse.

It is now necessary to enter the texts that hold statements of the Shi'a worldview for the Shi'a are noted for their unique blend of esoteric and exoteric Islamic practises, which are given focus and depth by a distinctly populist discourse.

The journey through the texts starts with "Islamic Government and the Revolution in Iran" by Ayatollah Allama Yahya Noori.

Ayatollah Noori states:

> "Concerning supervision over the government, the Prophet directed Muslims to obey their government only as far as it obeys God, and if its policies are based on Islam and not on the personal interests of the ruler. If rulers deviate from the divine law and act against the dictates of Islam, they forfeit their right to be obeyed and they are to be corrected and if necessary overthrown and replaced by a just government."

(Noori 1985 Page 25)

> "To combat oppression, to confront dictatorship and colonialism, to advise, to perform well and to avoid evil acts, to guide the people, to restore and expand the grounds of justice, to assist others in financial and moral matters etc are some of the social responsibilities of a Muslim."

(Noori 1985 Page 54)

"Therefore, Islam regards an enlightening fight against disbelief, non-believers and atheism as an obligation and also stresses much on expansion of Islamic society and Islamic brotherhood."

(Noori 1985 Page 54)

"On the other hand, it is the duty of a muslim not to befriend enemies of God and Islam and not to submit to the domination of atheists."

(Noori 1985 Page 54)

Ayatollah Noori expresses a worldview in its most potent form locked in battle with Western discourse. A flow of Islamic discourse so potent in its message to the Ummah that it has become locked in struggle for hegemony both within the Islamic discourse and with Western discourse.

The text "Modern Islamic Political Thought; the response of the Shi'i and Sunni Muslims to the 20th Century" by Hamid Enayat is an example of the attempts by Muslims to explain the rise of Shi'i populist radical Islam and its struggle for hegemony within Islamic discourse. A textual journey noted for its endless and repeated striving for understanding by a Muslim, of Muslim realities. Let us begin the journey as Enayat states:

"During the last two centuries Twelver Shi'ism in Iran, Iraq and Lebanon has displayed a political vitality, both in theory and practice, unprecedented in its long history. Shi'i vitality can be explained primarily by some of its potentialities for adaptation to social and political change."

(Enayat 1982 Page 160)

"The most essential of these are the principles of ijtihad or independent judgement, as a device supplementing the sources of the jurisprudence, and a potentially revolutionary power in the face of temporal power."

(Enayat 1982 Page 160)

"Only in Shi'ism is ijtihad the logical and imperative concomitant of the creed."

(Enayat 1982 Page 160)

"Far from indulging in the elaboration of barren jurisprudential schemes or anti-social esoterics, the "Ulama" thus appears to have done at least some preliminary work to turn their scholasticism into the service of the political cause of their people. Their realism tempered by a refusal to compromise on points of principle contrasts with their subsequent attitudes, which range from radical puritanism to opportunistic pacification."

(Enayat 1982 Page 174)

"However no amount of socio-political analysis of facts can account for the subtleties of thought processes. The historical background briefly described here can explain only the timing, but not the nature, of the new phase of Shi'i dynamism."

(Enayat 1982 Page 163)

Enayat recognizes the problematic of causal theorizing and moves from drawing out what for him are the essential differences between Shi'i and Sunni practises in Islamic discourse to a historical exposition of events to end with personal perceptions of the path of evolution followed by Twelver Shi'ism. He admits that causal theorizing cannot account for nor explain the paths thought processes follow as they are driven by bodies of perceptions. His text sought to textualize insights, to trap causalities to explain phenomena ensnared by the matrices of Enayat's field of knowledge.

He must be commended for his insight, his perceptions, which enabled him to "see" that the thought process that framed the phenomena ensnared evades, capture within the matrices that enclose space. He cannot explain the discourse of Shi'i Islam and its specific evolution, he can only map its co-ordinates, find and traverse its texts and by doing so deconstruct its discourse layer by layer. In the absence of texts he then has no other solution but to experience its esoterica through the only means possible sensory experiences. At the end of his enterprise as with all other enterprises driven by causality the circular dance of causal theorising continues for the perceptions, the base building blocks of thought processes remain the property of its human masters.

What is of relevance is the presentation of bodies of dualist concepts that drive the Shi'i worldview. These are:

al-amr bi al-ma'ruf wa al-nahy `an al-munkar/commend the good and forbid the bad.
Mustaz `afeen/the opressed
Mustakbereen/the oppressors.
Ijtihad/Ijma/Independent judgement/consensus of the believers.

And the discursive structures built upon the practice of Taqiyyah and the martyrdom of Husayn.Taqiyyah is the practice of concealment or dissimulation employed as a strategy of survival by Shi'i Islam. Over time structures of practises of taqiyyah have developed and discourses have developed charged with recognition and drawing out of practises of taquiyyah towards categorization and delimitation.

Therefore four major categories of taquiyyah are listed as predominant: (a) the enforced (ikrahiyyah), (b) precautionary or apprehensive (khawfiyyah), (c) arcane (kitmaniyyah) and (d) symbiotic (mutarati).

What taqiyyah allows is the ability to erect closed discourses to the exclusion of worldviews deemed in conflict with Shi'i Islamic discourse. Moreso it denies the link between language (written or spoken) and the expression of what is called truth or at best heart felt expressions. Taqiyyah exposes the reality of language, it fosters, it welcomes language deceptions, and it provides fertile grounds upon which it blossoms in a finely tuned system of language as a weapon of deconstruction. Taqiyyah gives space to language as deceiver, as the vehicle of "untruths" fostering its openness to the embrace of discourse. The text, the spoken word in Sufi'i Islam has then to be recognized for what it is; simply a means of expression and in no way is the text or the spoken word a vehicle for "truth".

Since the revolution of 1979 Taqiyyah has been the focus of a post-revolutionary move to re-definition (see Heikal 1981 Pgs. 136-137). The post-revolutionary perceptions have called for taqiyyah to be deemed outside of the realm of actions/communication directly related to the ortho praxis for Shi'i Islam. Taqiyyah is now deemed the consummate methodology of clandestine struggle and in this realm it retains its historical dominance as a framer of perceptions and action. Taqiyyah is now then excluded from the techniques of mass mobilisation of the Ummah, the responsibility for this lies in the principle of "commend the good and forbid the bad." It is obvious through the positions stated on taqiyyah that the discourse is now mutating to suit the reality that it now enjoys hegemonic dominance in Iran. Likewise the martyrdom of Husayn is being re-defined in the post-revolution realities of Iran.

Husayn's martyrdom is now being re-conceptualised as his actions are seen as the logical outcome of a worldview, which rejects a monarchist state based on hereditary succession. His actions were the result of his Islamic worldview hence it is and can be replicated throughout the history of Islam whenever Muslims heed the injunction to "command the good and forbid the bad". In Shi'i Islam in Iran since the revolution Husayn's martyrdom is gradually being perceived, interpreted, conceptualised no longer as a historical event of immutable epic proportions because of the blood line of Husayn but as the actions of a Muslim, any Muslim. The discourse is therefore positing martyrdom as the ultimate physically demonstrable human action in the ortho praxis of Shi'i Islam possible. The basis of this worldview is an esoteric asceticism that grounds the believer in an esoteric praxis of release.

Ayatollah Ruhollah Khumayni states on the martyrdom of Husayn as follows:

> "It was to prevent the establishment of monarchy and hereditary succession that Husayn revolted and became a martyr. It was for refusing to succumb to Yazid's hereditary succession and to recognize his kingship that Husayn revolted, and called all Muslims to rebellion."

(Enayat 1982 Page 194)

The discursive positioning of martyrdom since the revolution in Iran was aptly demonstrated during the Iran-Iraq conflict.

Enayat's text is therefore the clarion that issues the warning in the text to pilgrims on their journey through the Islamic discourse to never make the mistake and become entrapped in the enterprise of creating the illusory definitive text of causality on Islamic discourse. His text given his realization of the limits of his methodology can only beckon, via the road signs and mileposts he erected on the path he took in seeking out that elusive holy grail of western academic pursuits. His sign-posts are duly noted and recorded for they have been experienced by the researcher but the journey must continue and it must now enter the geographic spaces in which the researcher is spatially located.

The journey must now pass through texts that reflect the reality of being Muslim as a minority in a wider plural matrix normally termed the modern nation state. The text "Muslims Under Non-Islamic Law" by Fiazuddin Shu'ayb in The Torch of Islam, September 1991, presents the authors position on the contradiction that exists between Muslims and Western jurisprudence and proposals for resolving the contradiction in a non-violent manner.

Shu'ayb states:

> "What is the legal status of Muslim minorities under Jahili (non-Islamic law)? As far as we know there seems to be no definitive nor authoritative classification in the corpus of ancient or modern fiqhi (Islamic jurisprudence) literature."

> (Shu'ayb 1991 Page 8)

> "In contemporary history the variety of problems experienced by Muslim minorities is rooted in the non-existence of Dar-ul Islam, the lands which are under Islamic rule."

> (Shu'ayb 1991 Page 8)

> "The order out of this chaotic situation must be sought in the Shari'ah. The oversight of this crucial fact has led-or misled leaders of various Islamic movements to embrace positions as regards the Muslim minority's relationship with the non-Islamic state; from passivity to westernism on one hand, to radical militantness on the other."

> (Shu'ayb 1991 Page 8)

> "If Muslim minorities are no longer living in Dar-ul Islam does it mean that alternately they're living in Dar-ul Harb (that is hostile states or nations, which are at war with Dar-ul Islam whether de facto or de jure)?"

> (Shu'ayb 1991 Page 8)

"Research indicates that the conceptions of Dar-ul Islam and Dar-ul Harb are merely juristic expressions based on the traditional divisions held by the schools of laws (madhhubs) and not on express texts of the Shari'ah the sole source of legal authority in Islam."

(Shu'ayb 1991 Page 8)

"However the conception of Dar-ul Ahd, which means the non-Muslim states willing to live in peaceful relations with the Islamic state, is a juristic term for a status quo which did exist theoretically and practically and was based on Quranic texts for example Sura 8; 61."

(Shu'ayb 1991 Page 8)

"Thus the medium of treaty making with non-Islamic states or governments and the establishment of peaceful relations with them is, we declare, a valid legal position that could be adopted by some Muslim minorities."

(Shu'ayb 1991 Page 8)

"The legal position of Dar-ul Ahd should be adopted by the local Muslim community and be made its goal of establishing an autonomous Islamic political and economic entity in Trinidad and Tobago and, by extension the Caricom or Caribbean region."

(Shu'ayb 1991 Page 9)

Shu'ayb states his position by dismissing the pedigree of the dualist concepts of Dar-ul Islam/Dar-ul Harb by insisting that they are not of the Shar'iah thereby opening the door for his alternative position, which is in fact his worldview that some form of co-existence must be found and implemented. For Shu'ayb the solution is not a concordat or an accommodation but an autonomous entity, which seriously raises the question of the willingness of the ruling elites to set such a precedent in a deeply fractured society as Trinidad and Tobago.

But the lesson of the text is the fact that Islam does not conceptualise itself in a minority position in a non-Islamic state. The era of Dar-ul Ahd was but a fleeting movement in its history, which bore little relevance to the hegemony of the discourse that, blossomed within the first century of its existence. The hegemonic discourse simply does not address itself to the realities of an Islamic minority beached in a realm of unbelievers. The Muslim minorities, the castaways, are left to work out their non-discursive perceptions of their minority status and how to interact with the dominant non-Islamic discourses. Muslims in a minority position have by their texts, by their actions drawn upon various and at times contradictory discursive streams that form parts of Islamic discourse.

In the case of Trinidad and Tobago within the quantum of Muslims present two main trends have developed (a) the quietist/accomodationist discursive stream, which swings from syncretism to fundamentalist isolationism, (b) the radical/rejectionist stance that openly declares its alienation from non-Islamic discourse and its subsequent antagonism to/with non-Islamic discourse. The researchers journey through the historical texts have confirmed that the discursive structures formulated by Muslims in Trinidad in their bid to cope with their minority position both numerically and discursively, are not unique to Trinidad.

Muslims in minority discursive positions in the Indian sub-continent formulated a similar range of discursive structures of reaction, resistance and survival. (This will be expanded upon at another stage in the text.) The journey into the experiences of a Muslim minority and the discursive structures created to deal with their discursive subordination led to the text;"Muslim Minorities in the World Today" bu A.Ali Kettani (1986).

Kettani states:

> "Islam discourages a Muslim to acquiesce wilfully to a state of minority if he cannot exercise his right to worship the One True God."

> "Therefore when the right of a Muslim to practice his faith is denied by any power, he must either fight back in self defence, and become a mujahid; or if he cannot fight or fails in his fight; he should emigrate and become a muhajir. If he can do neither one nor the other, he should keep his faith, even secretly if he has to, and try his best to pass it on at least to his descendants."

> (Kettani 1986 Page 3)

"Indeed an Islamic definition of Muslim minority can be given as "those parts of the Muslim Ummah living outside its sovereignty." Indeed islamically the world is divided into three zones Dar-al-Islam (the land of Islam), Dar-al-Muahadah (the land of treaty) and Dar-al-Harb (the land of war).

(Kettani 1986 Pages 258-259)

"there are also two models for Muslim minorities to follow; one is the model of a Muslim minority in Dar-al-Harb and the other is for the Muslim minority in Dar-al-Muahadah."

"In the first case oppression led to warfare and eventually to the victory of truth over falsehood. In the second case, tolerance led to peaceful co-existence and exchange of ideas, making clear to everyone the truth from falsehood."

(Kettani 1986 Page 259)

Kettani's worldview within the discourse makes it clear that adherence to the discourse is paramount for that is what distinguishes the Muslim and creates the minority status to begin with. Syncretism is not a solution within the discourse, Muslims in a minority position faced with a situation perceived as hostile to a Muslim minority have either to fight/to run and to die for to turn from the faith is shirk. These are the only solutions forwarded by the discourse to Muslim minorities who perceive that the unbelievers, the kuffir, are intent on destroying Muslims.

Martyrdom is then the preferred solution to the difficulties of being Muslim in an openly hostile anti-muslim society. For it means that muslims die within the faith untainted by Shirk, liberated from the physical condition of being human and once more existing in unison with Allah. The relevance of the model of Dar-al-Muahadah lies in the existence of a non-hostile, non-believing entity who is willing to recognize the need of the Muslim to be centred within the ortho-praxis of the discourse. In the Islamic discourse there can be no treaty with any un-believing entity, which refuses to allow, to enable Muslims to be Muslims i.e. to animate the Islamic praxis.

In keeping with the fact that compromises with the praxis of the discourse are shirk it then becomes obvious that the model of treaty has limited relevance for there is no need for treaty between muslims and unbelievers if the minority muslim is being allowed to implement and adhere to Islamic praxis. Furthermore, whenever a treaty exists between Muslims and unbelievers it does not obviate the need for jihad nor does it exclude it, whenever the treaty is invalidated by actions of the unbelievers. Shu'ayb therefore recognizes the inherent weakness of his position by positing the model of treaty as the option sanctioned by Shari'ah for dealing with unbelievers. For the Qur'an sanctions both models of action therefore leaving it up to the ummah to decide upon which model of action to resort to in the face of perceived hostility by unbelievers.

Shu'ayb therefore has to add dimensions to his solution, which raise questions of its relevance, and applicability to the post-colonial realities of Trinidad and Tobago. He has to believe in this Muslim enclave; this entity within Caricom for to him its existence, recognized under treaty, would be the Caribbean's version of another Pakistan. The safe haven for the Muslim minorities of the Caribbean thereby obviates the need to resort to his greatest fear, jihad. For he is convinced that conflicts would continually arise between Muslims and the unbelievers and in the face of such conflict the discourse does not enjoin its adherents to pacifism. The nightmare continually haunts the consciousness of the accomodationatist/pacifist stream of Islam in Trinidad. They live in dread of the day when they would be drawn into a conflict with unbelievers primarily due to two developments;(a) the outbreak of hostilities between the unbelievers and the radical/rejectionist stream of the discourse. (b) If the unbelievers were to openly adopt hostile stances and carry out acts of aggression against the accomodationist/pacifist stream of the discourse. Muslims of this worldview in Trinidad are forever cursed to be continually on the alert, to be ever watchful for signs of the impending anti-muslim pogroms of the unbelievers.

Developments in international sections of the ummah visibly heighten the tension such as the anti-muslim genocide of Bosnia-Hercegovina and the pogroms of India. The attempted coup d'etat of the Jamaat al Muslimeen on July 27th 1990 was therefore perceived as the catalyst to the long awaited anti-muslim holocaust in Trinidad. The accomodationist/pacifist stream of the discourse has in reaction created specific discursive positions to deal with the post coup d'etat realities as have the radical stream of the discourse. (These would be handled in some depth in other areas of the text.)

Muslim minorities in states under the hegemony of non-Islamic discourses are offered two discursive structures by Shi'i Islam, which are of relevance in their search for instruments which foster their repeated actions to come to grips with the realities of their subservient discursive positions. These discursive structures are taqiyyah and the martyrdom of Husayn. A Muslim who is in a perceptually besieged position in the power relations of a non-Islamic society can apply the strategic techniques of taqiyyah towards ensuring that the power relations, which enmeshes the said Muslim, guile, cunning and deception become associated with interactions with muslims.

Taqiyyah enables Muslims as a specific entity within the power relations of any given structure to forge coalitions across the contradictions of the clash between Islamic and non-Islamic discourse. Taqiyyah focuses the gaze of any given Muslim minority on the only relevant task as a besieged body of believers i.e. survival of the Ummah, thereby opening the door for entry into any and all realms of the power relations of a given entity, which impacts upon the struggle for survival of the Ummah. Ultimately taqiyyah as a discursive structure enables a Muslim to place his ortho praxis into segregated realms of relevance, which ensure the survival of the discourse.

Thus in dealings with enemies of Islam the muslim is not hindered nor fettered by the moral structures of the discourse for simply an enemy of Islam, is an enemy of Allah therefore kuffir. The enemy of Allah by his actions cannot be the beneficiary, nor does he deserve to be, of the moral structures of Allah. In dealings with unbelievers in an environment perceived as hostile to Muslims the worldview simply teaches survival by any means necessary.

The discursive structures, which enmesh the martyrdom of Husayn in Shi'i Islam, are of significance to Muslim minorities who situate themselves within the stream characterized by radical, confrontationist stances with non-Islamic discourses. Shi'i Islam posits Husayn's martyrdom as a model of Muslim action in the face of shirk. The discursive structures of martyrdom constantly seek to motivate Muslims to action by insisting that it is incumbent upon Muslims to resist to the point of death discursive positions/structures, which threaten the hegemony of Islam with Godlessness or Jahiliyya. To Muslims trapped within non-Islamic discourses who perceive that their worldview is under threat moreso faced with extinction the Shi'i Islamic discourse mutates to fit their perceived realities.

As the contradictions between the minority Islamic discourse and the hegemonic non-Islamic discourses heighten muslim perceptions which accept the validity and desirability of violent confrontation are afforded the discourse of martyrdom by the Islamic discourse as a possible worldview through which the muslim comes to grip with, prepares his or herself for the perceived realities of violent confrontation, the most potent of which is death. The discourse of martyrdom constitutes subjects who view their act of confrontation as their final and ultimate action in the ortho praxis of Islam. Their death is a secondary result of the power relations of violent contradiction, a simple aside for their death is a result of submission to Allah's will (Islam). By their ultimate act of submission death opens the means to entry into paradise. Moreso, their act of submission summed up in their death attests, by their example to the Muslims still alive, the potency of Islamic discourse. Taqiyyah and martyrdom are then two potentially devastating discursive structures open and available to Muslim minorities the world over to be utilised in the discursive conflicts with the hegemonic non-Islamic discourses with which they are locked in contradiction.

At this instance in the text the researcher must now present portraits of his journey through the single authoritative text in the Islamic discourse: the Qur'an. The researcher experienced the textual perspectives, the worldviews textualized and presented as instances of a journey in the preceding text. But the entire exercise is irrelevant without presentation of the researcher's journey through the Qur'an. In this specific context the researcher experienced the Qur'an seeking discursive structures, which came into play whenever the text was consulted by any believer in search of answers/markers/pointers towards solving the perceptually constituted problems of being Muslim in a hostile environment. The following textualised instances jump out of the text and reverberate perceptually, it is left up to the reader to act upon the text or seek alternate texts, which provide an alternate worldview.

These are:

> "God hath purchased of the Believers
> Their persons and their goods; For theirs Is the garden;
> They fight in this cause, and slay and are slain;
> A promise binding on him In Truth, through the law
> The Gospel, and the Qur'an
> And who is more faithful to his covenant than God?
> Then rejoice in the bargain, which ye have concluded,
> That is the achievement supreme.

> (Glorious Qur'an Sura ix: 111)

God hath promised to Believers, Men and Women, Gardens
Under which rivers flow, to dwell therein,
And beautiful mansions in Gardens of everlasting bliss.
But the greatest bliss is the Good Pleasure of God;
That is the supreme felicity.

(Glorious Qur'an Sura ix. 72)

Say, "Can you expect for us Other than one of two glorious things-
(Martyrdom or victory)?
But we can expect for you either that God will send his punishment
from himself, or by our hands.
So wait, we too will wait with you."

(Glorious Qur'an Sura ix. 52)

O ye who believe! What is the matter with you?
That, when ye are asked to go forth in the Cause of God,
Ye cling heavily to the earth?
Do ye prefer the life of this world to the Hereafter?
But little is the comfort of this life, as compared with the Hereafter.

(Glorious Qur'an Sura ix. 38)

Those who believe and suffer exile and strive with might
And main, in God's cause with their goods and their persons,
Have the highest rank in the sight of God,
They are the people who will achieve.

(Glorious Qur'an Sura ix. 20)

Fight them, and God will punish them by your hands,
Cover them with shame, help you over them,
Heal the breasts of Believers.

(Glorious Qur'an Sura ix. 14)

O Apostle! rouse the Believers to the fight.
If there are twenty amongst you; patient

And persevering, they will vanquish two hundred; if a hundred
They will vanquish a thousand of the unbelievers; for these
Are a people without understanding.

>(Glorious Qur'an Sura viii. 65)

And fight them on until there is no more Tumult or oppression,
And there prevail Justice and faith in God altogether and everywhere;
But if they cease, verily God doth see all that they do.

>(Glorious Qur'an Sura viii. 39)

If a wound hath touched you, be sure a similar wound
Hath touched the others.
Such days we give to men and men by turns; that God may know
Those that believe, and that he may take;
To Himself from your ranks Martyr-witnesses
And God loved not those that do wrong.

>(Glorious Qur'an Sura iii. 140)

The ontology of being in the texts quoted above insists that man in submission to Allah must be willing, able and ready to make the ultimate sacrifice for Islam. But moreso, the texts insist that there is no submission in the Islamic discourse to Jahiliyya. It is simply inconceivable in the discourse to contemplate a state of existence in which Islam has submitted to, has been conquered by a state of Godlessness, of atheistic anarchy/Jahiliyya. When faced with such a possible outcome of aggression between Islamic and non-Islamic discourse the Muslim is provided with the final solution to submission to Jahiliyya i.e. martyrdom through armed violent conflict.

Jihad is then a multi-faceted discursive structure for it insists that the discourse must defend itself when attacked physically by the kuffir. Jihad the discursive structure refuses to be re-defined into irrelevance within the discourse, for it is the defining structure that provides perceptual worldviews whenever Muslims in positions of subordination to kufirs seek solutions of the discourse, the path to liberation. The Palestinian Intifada is but another example of the discursive structures of Jihad, in the discourse as it constitutes objects of knowledge imbued with the "soul" of martyrdom.

For it is martyrdom that constitutes the body of the martyr; an object of knowledge. It is martyrdom that constitutes the "soul" that drives the discursive process that constitutes martyrs, that inhabits and embodies the person who is the martyr. It is this "soul" that enables the replication of the discursive structures through linear time for it is driven by a specific ontological worldview. This concept of being insists that man is of God in the image and likeness of the Absolute it is therefore ontological suicide to conceive of man being able to attain their fullest potential in a state of existence alienated from the Absolute.

In this ontology there is for man no alternative to Islam for the dualist opposite of Islam is for man not an opposite. To reject Islam is to deny that man is the reflection of the Absolute on the level of the finite. To reject Islam is to deny the genesis of man and their ability, uniquely theirs, for God realization. To reject Islam is then to descend to the realm of bestiality, to subject man to a level of existence for which they were never created. The discourse does not posit a duality of existences in opposition, the ontology refuses to accept the viability of the opposite whilst recognizing the potency of its attraction to mankind.

Islam's ortho praxis is therefore determined by its ontology for the ortho praxis insists upon practises which discipline and punish the body ensuring through praxis that both the body and the mind are kept spatially located within the sphere of Islam therefore away from the spaces under the hegemonic dominance of Jahiliyyah.

The ontology of the discourse therefore "sees," "gazes" upon bodies that must be molded, to be disciplined, to be punished, to be spatially positioned within the discursive spaces of an ortho praxis that stresses discipline and submission through a repetitive praxis of denial.

Moreso the discourse creates a community of believers, the ummah, who embody the ortho praxis, who replicate the discourse and ensure the hegemony of the ortho-praxis. For in Islam there is no intermediary between Allah and humankind, there is therefore no priesthood, no mediator, no Christ. In the absence of the intermediaries between Allah and man, Islam was never and cannot ever be burdened with interpretators of the text, with catechisms, with a Papacy. Orthodoxy in Islam therefore does not exist; there are only the five pillars and the Shari'ah, which is law, the basis of the ortho-praxis applied to the daily lives of the Muslim.

The Shari'ah deepens, extends the "gaze" of the discourse as it reaches into the daily practises of the Muslim, it moulds perceptions at the specificities of each individual locked in an ortho-praxis. The Shari'ah is then the policing agency of the ortho-praxis, the pan optican of mirrors in, through and by which the praxis of every muslim is constituted, monitored, "gazed" upon," seen" and reflected upon by the individuals who make up the "Ummah". The question then arises of how does the discourse police the praxis-praxis in nation states where non-muslim law is hegemonic and the sharpie is reduced to a heavily encumbered and limited agency in the operations of the Islamic discourse?

The Ummah can only apply the Shari'ah in spatial niches heavily encumbered by the rule of hegemonic kuffir law. The contradiction between the Shari'ah and kuffir law especially Western capitalist, nationalist law is blatantly antagonistic and a constant struggle is waged for hegemony, the power to police the ortho-praxis of the discourse. It is apparent to the ummah that whenever Western capitalist law penetrates the discourse and abrogates, seizes the right to police the ortho-praxis of the discourse, the discourse inevitably begins to fall apart at the seams and syncretism abounds. Western capitalist law as it seizes the power to police the ortho-praxis, systemically sets about the deconstruction of the discourse through lopping off the discursive links that enabled the "gaze", the constituting of the object of knowledge.

A Muslim minority faced with such a reality has simply to work out its own salvation on an individual basis. But the Ummah as a constituted agglomeration, an aggregation of the ortho-praxis throws up various tendencies of reaction and resistance. What is basic to tendencies de-limited and studied by the researcher is the search for individual, personal solutions that foster, promote survival and some modicum of retention of the Islamic discourse. The polar opposites span syncretism to martyrdom. The resilience and effectiveness of the ortho-praxis in constituting adherents is attested to by the extremely low level of persons who walk away from the discourse when faced with a choice of life or death.

Syncretism created by combining Islamic discourse with instances of discursive and extra-discursive practises, has always been a reality in the discourse for it stresses an ortho-praxis policed through law. Various discourses and extra-discursive worldviews have been absorbed into the ortho-praxis with apparent ease. Syncretism for Islamic discourse occurs when discursive and extra-discursive praxis becomes hegemonic thereby pushing away the praxis-praxis of the discourse. Whenever this has in fact happened the discourse has always responded with revivals, rebirths sparked by specific leaders who founded movements for renewal and revival. But with reference to the opposite pole, which is, situated within a worldview within the discourse that perceptually determines that the most viable solution to the contradiction between kuffir discourse and Islamic discourse is violent engagements built upon Jihad.

How does the ummah respond to this specific worldview within the discourse? How does, specifically, the Ummah in a minority position in a nation state dominated by Western discourse respond to Muslims who adopt such a pathway of resistance? But moreover how do Muslims perceptually adopt Jihad as a strategy of resistance and in doing so what are the structures of their action as Mujahid? Before we delve into this perceptive catalyst of action and the structures that animate the perceptions, the researcher must present texts, which addressed the ontological necessity of the Shari'ah and the ortho-praxis of Islamic discourse.

The text is drawn from "Towards Understanding Islam" by Sayyid Abul Ala Mawdudi. Mawdudi speaking on the Shari'ah states:

> "The scheme of life which Islam envisages consists of a set of rights and obligations, and every human being, everyone who accepts this religion, is enjoined to live up to them."

> (Mawdudi 1981 Page 110)

> "These rights and obligations constitute the corner-stone of Islam and it is the duty of every true Muslim to understand them and obey them earnestly and carefully. The Shari'ah clearly discusses each and every right and deals with it in detail. It also throws light on the ways and means through which the obligations can be discharged-so that all of them may be simultaneously implemented and none of them gets violated or trampled underfoot."

> (Mawdudi 1981 Page 110)

> "Broadly speaking, the law of Islam imposes four kinds of rights and obligations upon every man viz (1) the rights of God, which

every man is obliged to fulfil, (2} his own rights upon his own self, (3) the rights of other people over him, (4) the rights of those powers and resources, which God has placed in his service…"

The Rights of God

"The most primary and foremost right of God is that man should have faith in him alone."

"The second right of God on us is to accept whole heartedly and follow his guidance (Hidayat)-the code he has revealed for man-and to seek his pleasure with all the biddings of the mind and soul."

(Mawdudi 1981 Page 110)

"The third right of God on us is that we should obey him honestly and unreservedly. We fulfil the needs of this right by following God's law as contained in the Qur'an and the Sunnah."

"The fourth right of God on us is to worship him."

"These rights and obligations precede all other rights and as such they are discharged even at the cost of some sacrifice of other rights and duties."

"And in Jihad he sacrifices money, material and all that he has-even his own life."

"Similarly, in the discharge of these obligations one has to sacrifice, more or less, some of the ordinary rights of others and thus injure his own interests at large."

"In Jihad a man takes away life and gives it away solely in the cause of Allah. In the same way, in rendering God's rights one has to sacrifice many of those things which man has in his control, like animals, wealth, etc."

(Mawdudi 1981 Page 111)

"The greatest sacrifice in the way of God is made in Jihad, for in it a man sacrifices not only his own life and property in his cause but destroys those of others also. But, as already stated, one of the Islamic principles is that we should suffer a lesser loss to save ourselves from a greater loss.
What comparison can the loss of some lives-even if they are some thousands or more-bear to the calamity that may befall mankind as a result of the victory of evil over good and of aggressive atheism over the religion of God. Decidedly that is a much greater loss and a bigger calamity, for as a result of it not only the religion of God will run down but the world will also become the abode of evil immoralities and perversion, and life will be disrupted from within and without. In order to escape this greater evil God has, therefore commanded us to sacrifice our lives and property for his pleasure."

(Mawdudi 1981 Pages 112-113)

Mawdudi defines Jihad as such:

"Jihad is a part of this overall defence of Islam. Jihad means struggle to the utmost of one's capacity. A man who exerts himself physically or mentally or spends his wealth in the way of Allah is indeed engaged in Jihad. But in the language of the Shari'ah this word is used particularly for the war that is waged solely in the name of Allah and against those who perpetrate oppression as enemies of Islam. This supreme sacrifice devolves on all Muslims. If, however, a section of the Muslims offer themselves for participating in the Jihad, and the whole community is absolved of its responsibility. But if none comes forward, everybody is guilty."

(Mawdudi 1981 Page 100)

"In all these cases, Jihad is as much a primary duty of the Muslims concerned as are the daily prayers or fasting. One who shirks it is a sinner. His very claim to being a Muslim is doubtful. He is plainly a hypocrite who fails in the test of sincerity and all his "Ibadat" and prayers are a sham, a worthless hollow show of devotion."

(Mawdudi 1981 Page 101)

Mawdudi's text throws up the ontology that drives the ortho-praxis in turn indicating the hegemony of ortho-praxis. Jihad is the ultimate manifestation of the ortho-praxis in which Muslims through the ortho-praxis of denial and sacrifice now create the hegemony of God thereby enabling the Muslim to answer in the affirmative all the dictates of God. Jihad is then the ultimate test, the crucible of the ortho-praxis and of relevance to all Muslims for Mawdudi would perceive it no other way. For him Islamic discourse is not quietest, pacifist nor accomodationatist for the basis of the discourse is disciplining, channelling the sinful nature of man to enable the blossoming of man's godly legacy through submission to God's law.

Islamic discourse is then interventionist, activist, as it constantly seeks and thrives on hegemony both inward and outward. The Jihad of the inward state must be complemented, supplemented and bolstered by Jihad of the outward state and vice versa. For Mawdudi, a muslim must rejoice in the conjuncture in which he is called up to embrace Jihad for it is the most glorious test of his submission to Allah.

Such is Mawdudi's embrace of Jihad that he insists that it is located within the Shari'ah hence a structure of the praxis-praxis of Islamic discourse. Thereby his insistence that all Muslims and their actions in the face of contradictions with Jahih'yya are obligated to utilise the Jihad as structured by the Shari'ah. For Mawdudi Jihad is therefore an obligation upon the Muslims for it is a right of God.

At this juncture in the journey of the researcher as the texts are put down in tracts of written language it is now necessary to switch gears, to enter into unexplored territory. The researcher would now present the textual representations of the researchers experiences of the texts of pilgrimage, which dealt with instances of a Muslim minority's utilisation of Jihad to resolve contradictions with non-Muslim majorities. The two primary instances that beckoned to the researcher were/are situated geographically in the Indian sub-continent and the Philippines. The texts journeyed through are all historical accounts of the unfolding of Jihad, severely limited for the pursuits of the researcher but one has to work with what one has.

The most severe limitation of the texts is the fact that there are few accounts/texts presented of the Muslims in Jihad. In both the Indian and Philippine realities the Muslims in Jihad in effect remain silenced by the ruling discourses of the day i.e. textually but there is action, there is expression, there is defiance, there is refusal to remain oppressed and silenced. The Muslims in both instances chose to speak volumes of their discourse through violent actions, their martyrdom that reverberates without words but with the sounds of the pyrotechnics of death through the history of the silenced of the periphery. The Muslims in both instances therefore did not need to leave texts to their martyrdom, to the researcher what they did leave through their martyrdom was the challenge to understand, to feel, to experience, the discursive structures which replicates through history the discursive structures that constitute a mujahid, an object of knowledge and a sovereign subject who accepts the inevitability of death and by so doing embraces death by deliberately carrying out acts of violence which can only ensure his death.

The Orientalist West continues to cry out in racist alarm that these are but actions of mindless fanatics spawned by an imperialist religion. For the researcher the drive to understand, to experience lay in the fact that the discourse carried within its structures a warrior worldview that was spatially defined and embraced within the concept of Jihad. Within this warrior worldview as in all warrior ethics such as Bushido of Japan and the Dog Soldiers of the Lakota, a specific approach to and definition of death pervades the worldview and it is the primary motivator to violent action. Islamic discourse has embraced and absorbed a warrior ethic, which it draws upon in times of challenge and contradiction from without the discourse.

The process of constituting the Muslim warrior, the structures of perception through which he views or viewed the world and the linkages between perception and action are the primary interests of the researcher. This is in itself another body of work to be done in the future, the reality for the text of this moment is to present the experiences of the historical text, ever looking towards the moment in the text when the discourse of the Jamaat al Muslimeen would become the central instance of the text being laid down by the researcher.

The text spotlighted on a specific body of experiences of Muslims in a minority situation is "Islamic Society on the South Asian Frontier. The Mapillas of Malabar 1498-1922" by Stephen Frederic Dale (Dale 1980). Since 1984 this text has slept on the open shelves of the UWI Main library only to be reawakened, to be made relevant to the discourses of the University by the events of July 27th 1990. The attempted coup of July 27th 1990 therefore gave this text the attention it now commands for in our search for understanding of the events of the events of July 27th 1990 the Academic discourses are scouring the texts seeking that elusive holy grail.

A most fitting summation of the enterprise of academia devoid of praxis for it is a circular dance of discourse for itself, by itself and in itself, the discourse constitutes a stream of objects of knowledge trapped within a largely irrelevant corpus of power relations for these power relations simply cannot change the price of cocoa. This is itself the reality of Dale's work but moreso it is unapologetically blatantly Orientalist and by extension racist in its worldview. Dale speaks through his text thus:

> "Finally the rebellion was emphatically not a modern political event, even though it occurred in the 20th century. Quite the contrary, the rebellion like the mutiny, was essentially an archaic form of protest, as it offered no viable political alternative for the future. In this respect the closest 19th century analogy to the Ma'ppila Rebellion was not the mutiny but rather the attempt, which Sayyid Ahmad Barelvi and his mujahidu'n made to establish an Islamic state in the Punjab in the late 1820's. Here was an attempt by a man whose religious outlook closely resembled that of Sayyid Fadl, to resuscitate Indian Islam by founding a theocratic kingdom. With virtually no planning the Mappilas attempted to achieve the same goal for themselves in 1921,how much more archaic the Ma'pilla effort seemed almost a century after Sayyid Ahmad Barelvi had failed in the Punjab."

(Dale 1980 Pages 217-218)

It is tiresome to continually point out the racist assumptions that pervades the "white man's" texts as they repeatedly pour scorn upon all our "failed" attempts to unseat their hegemony in our history of colonial domination.

Dale's worldview is not uniquely his for the same dismissal of the futility of rebellion against western hegemony, the language that harangues our exercises in futile rebellion is found throughout their orientalist texts. The language that harangues, that tears at our sensibilities as a dominated people as the talons of an eagle on its prey, comes back at us in the texts that dealt with the Jamaat al Muslimeen and the events of July 27th 1990. Need we say no more on Dale's enterprise for having located the ontological centre of his worldview nothing we experience in the text should rankle the researcher. Dale defines his enterprise as follows:

"This work is a study in frontier history. It is a study of how two frontiers shaped the modern history of the Muslims of Kerala, the oldest Islamic community in the South Asian sub continent. It is a study of how Kerala Muslims' confrontation with European powers on the one hand and the predominantly Hindu Kerala society on the other evolved an Islamic community whose most prominent cultural characteristic was religious militancy."

"These attacks all shared a common feature; the Ma'pillas carried them out as Jihads, as wars for the faith, and those who participated intentionally martyred themselves at the conclusion of each assault."

(Dale 1980 Page 1)

Dale is therefore positing that the frontier created with European conquest of Kerala directly influenced the development of the focus of conflict generated by the hegemony of European colonialism. He posits:

"Kerala became an Islamic frontier in 1498 when Malayali Muslims shared in the monopoly of the Arabian Sea spice trade."

(Dale 1980 Page 2)

"In 1498 the Portuguese discovered the principal Indian spice entrepot at Calicut..."

"Thus not only did the Portuguese seek to usurp the spice trade, but they were also eager to exterminate Islamic communities whenever the opportunity arose."

"The Portuguese attempt to achieve these goals in Kerala provoked an appropriately militant response on the part of Malayali Muslims, which eventually became an indelible trait of Islamic society in Kerala..."

"Malayali Muslims perceived this struggle in traditional Islamic terms as Jihad, but the situation of Muslims in Kerala as a politically subordinate, mercantile community meant that the jihad assumed a special character there. In most Islamic societies where Muslims were sovereign jihads were used as a weapon of the state, to be postponed or abandoned if success seemed unlikely, but in Kerala Muslims were a minority with no ruler to defend them as they were besieged by a succession of European, Christian powers and in 1792 subjugated to the last of those antagonists, the British East India Company."

(Dale 1980 Page 3)

Dale viewing the actions of Malayali Muslims speaks about the choice of Jihad as a solution to the contradictions as a traditional choice. What other choice does Dale expect the Muslims to have made save and except that of departing from, exiting of the discursive spaces thrown up by Islamic discourse? For within the discourse the range of actions open to muslims were all already enumerated and the lesson of the Malayali muslims was the use of Jihad as an ongoing continuous method of resistance through the creation of specific discursive structures that constituted a spatial specificity occupied only by the mujahidin.

The Malayali Muslims created a warrior order open to all male muslims who upon volunteering for entry into the order, specific discursive structures unique to the task of replicating and constituting the specific warrior person operated within and upon the space and the objects of knowledge constituted within; the Mujahidin. In a dance with death and the space created within the embrace of death the discourse created the language of death and martyrdom, which defeated death, for death was the access point to eternal bliss in the Gardens of Paradise.

Unlike Dale the researcher's position is that the Malayali Muslims did not in fact resort to traditional structures to resolve contradictions. What they did in fact is evolve the discourse, to expand its relevance, its applicability, its range of perceptive structures encoded for future users to suit the needs of the worldview of specific Muslims then in Kerala and in the future for the martyrdom of Kerala muslims does not stand as an isolated, irrelevant response mechanism within the history of the discourse.

With or without cross-fertilization the weapon of martyrdom continues to be wielded within the Islamic discourse. There are therefore no causal inferences of instrumentalities to seek out and create from the experiences and actions of Malayali Muslims. Dale insists that it is because of the minority status of the Malayali Muslims that Jihad developed into suicidal acts. Why then the suicidal acts of Shi'i Muslims in Iran during the revolution of 1979? Why then the suicidal truck bombing of the American embassy in Beirut? Why then the suicidal acts of the Palestinian Intifada?

Dale states:

> "This explains why in Kerala the jihad, normally the tactic of an expanding state, became a suicidal act, an expression of desperation and defeat."

> (Dale 1980 Page 3)

Dale's racist worldview is expected and as a result he cannot understand much less feel the psychic trauma of colonial domination, for he has never lived domination.

The simple fact of the matter is that martyrdom became a distinct discursive structure within Islamic discourse with the advent of European colonial capitalist domination.

For it was in this era that the Islamic discourse did not command the required technologies of death to overcome the colonial armies on the colonial killing fields of the periphery. Faced with the technological superiority of the "White Man" the discourse resisted to the point of martyrdom and never failed to resist thereby welcoming martyrdom. The discursive structures that constituted the mujahidin in the period of colonial domination were the product of the contradictions of the colonial clash between Islamic and Western discourses. By resisting to the point of martyrdom the discourse revitalised itself, it expanded its internally generated mechanisms to be always relevant to the demands placed upon the discourse by its adherents.

The suicidal actions of the mujahidin created space won from the western discourse within which the Islamic discourse constituted its objects of knowledge, replicated its matrices of knowledge and expanded them to penetrate extra discursive awakenings on the outer peripheries of the discourse. Whenever the space won by the mujahidin always under threat by the hegemonic discourse began to shrink as its perimeters folded under the pressure of the assault of Western discourse, Muslims perceiving the shrinking space would then choose to respond through re-awakening and creation of initiates to the order of the Mujahidin. For the Malayali Muslims various signs of assault were perceived as breaches of the perimeters of their Islamic space such as Hindu landlord evictions of low caste Hindus who became Muslims, or the policies implemented by the British Raja, which sought to subvert the Shari'ah.

The text of representations by Dale must at this stage be scoured for texts created by the martyrs for it is their discourse we are primarily interested in. He reproduces the testimony of a mujahid who survived his attack on a Hindu landlord during an outbreak in 1885. The text speaks:

> "I had heard that there was a reward in heaven for those who got shot after killing a kafir. A man about our place became a sabid (sic). His name was Ali. This was 4 or 5 years ago. Then I was told of the reward. Ali had killed a cheruman and was coming against the Pisharodi (the Nambutri janmi) when he was shot. It was the same Pisharodi that I killed. I thought that I should meet the same fate as Ali. I had the reward in view in what I did. When Ali went out to commit the offence he asked me to join. I did not join him because he used to beat me when my cattle trespassed. Ali killed the Cheruman because he broke the religion. I do not know why he went against the Pisharodi. I have heard that my brother-in-law Hydru, was ejected by the Pisharodi 2 or 3 years ago. I never asked anyone to join me. I did not take a blessing or anything, or tell anyone what I was going to do."

> (Dale 1980 Page 100)

The British official taking this statement had no means to determine "truth" from "falsehood" in the statement. The contents of the statements would have the desired effect for the admission of guilt in the murder of the landlord meant that death by hanging was inevitable for the Muslim mujahid. The covert value of the statement to the British Raj is dubious at best for the Muslim insists he was never initiated into the warrior order and his actions were solely influenced by memories of the actions of Ali his neighbour.

What is indicative of the debilitating effect of racism on its practitioners is their gullibility when receiving the "texts" of the people of the periphery conveyed orally or written. Dale is actually taken in by the text of the warrior as he purports causalities from the text of the warrior. He is blinkered by his worldview for he cannot impute to the text of the warrior the fact that it is the product of war by other means, a product of the discursive structure of taqiyyah. The next text Dale gave textual space to was one of the numerous war songs of the mujahidin still prevalent in Malayali culture today. It states:

> "The soul in our body is in the hands of God. Can we live forever in this world? Must we not die once? Everything will die but God alone will not. Such being the commandment of God we will have no excuse when we are brought to him after death; so determine earnestly to fight and die. If we die fighting with the wicked men who attempt to forcibly burn this holy mosque, which is the house of God, we shall obtain complete salvation. The occasion to fight and die for the faith is like unto embracing in a vessel, which has come to bear the believer to the shores of bliss. Therefore embark! The pleasure of wealth or family is not equal to an atom of celestial happiness. Our most venerable Prophet has said that those who die in battle can see the houris who will come to witness the fight. There is nothing in this world to compare with the beauty of the houris. The splendour of the sun, of the moon, and the lightning is darkness compared with the beauty of their hair, which hangs over their shoulders. Their cheeks, eyes, face, eyebrows, forehead are incomparably lovely. Their lips are like corals.... their breasts like cups of gold...Gently touch the wounds of those who die in battle they rub away the blood and cure the pain; they kiss and embrace the martyrs, give them to drink of the sweet water and gratify their every wish."

> (Dale 1980 Page 133)

There have been no text discovered which give insights into the practises of the order mujahidin, some clarity is afforded by texts from the Philippines, experiences of the mujahid in the south of the Philippine archipelago. Dale quotes:

> "On the eve of the day set for the performance of the duty, the mujahid (the presumptive shahid) was completely shaved of his hair and eyebrows. He then went through a complete ritual bathing as a symbol of purification followed by dressing completely in white. Sometimes he wore a small white turban. The colour here is

that of mourning and the clothing signified the burial shroud. The mujahid would spend the evening in prayer."

(Dale 1980 Page 59)

The modus operandi of the attacks of the mujahidun rendered their acts unique for they would carry out their attacks upon the targets chosen, then retreat to a designated assembly point such as a house, temple or mosque and calmly await the arrival of the military forces of the hegemonic colonial power. With the arrival of the troops they would then attack the military forces repeatedly armed only with short swords until dead. The act of repeated assaults upon a superior military force until rendered dead was to have the salient impact upon the minds of all social groupings locked in contradiction with Malayali Muslims in Kerala. The British summed up the Malayali Muslim as follows:

> "The Moplah is an obstinate ruffian. Cases are quoted of a culprit spitting in the face of a judge when the warrant of execution was being read to him." (Richard Burton, Goa and the Blue Mountains P.233)
>
> (Dale 1980 Page 119)

> "The pride and intolerance of the Mahomedan faith, coupled with the grasping, treacherous and vindictive character of the Mopplah's, in these districts drawn out to its worst extent, have fomented the evil, and it may be said to lie at the root thereof."
>
> (Dale 1980 Page 160)

> "Any real attempt to control religious teaching and preaching would be viewed as persecution, and we should have sedition preached on the hill tops, in the depths of the jungle, in the dens and holes of the earth." (H.M.Winterbotham 5/5/1896).
>
> (Dale 1980 Page 153)

The journey through Dale's text is ending and the researcher has experienced from the hidden text the growth and development of a specific discursive structure of the periphery created and developed in response to the need of the Islamic discourse in a minority demographic position to respond in survival mode to the attacks of hostile anti-Islam Western colonialist discourse.

In the case of Kerala, Malayali Muslims faced with the genocide of a rampant, racist Islamophobic Portuguese mercantilist colonialism the discourse was set on its path, which culminated in the creation of the warrior code amongst a minority Muslim population. Likewise the brutal onslaughts of Spanish colonialism on the Muslim of the Philippines noted for its genocide and Islamophobia was to create the very same phenomena of the warrior code. The warrior code would develop and become a hegemonic discursive structure spanning Spanish, American and Japanese colonialism and surviving to the 1990's.

In the course of the researcher's journey through the text by Dale it was discovered that Dale was positing that Kerala and the Philippines were linked by the common genesis of their Islamic minorities and the prolonged battle with Western colonialism. Dale states his case as follows:

> "In both Sumatra and the muslim regions of the southern Philippines centuries of defensive and ultimately unsuccessful warfare evolved the same tradition of suicidal jihad's as developed in Kerala. Then too, in the Philippines as in Kerala the prolonged struggle between Europeans and Muslims eventually led to the growth of a modern separatist movement."

(Dale 1980 Page 9)

The researcher had then but one choice that was to pursue the trail to the Philippines and more specifically to the history of Muslim's in the Philippines. Dale himself says the following:

> "For their part Philippine Muslims perceived the conflict in exactly the same terms as Zayn al Din and the Atjehnese, as an attack by kafirs on the dar al-Islam, in which Muslims were obliged to undertake the jihad in their own defence. As the Spanish gradually extended their authority, Philippine Muslims in Sulu and elsewhere

began to resort to suicidal attacks; those who did so were known to the Spanish as "juramentado", one who takes an oath, and to the Muslims themselves as "sabil ullah", those who fought in the way of God."

(Dale 1980 Pages 58-59)

Dale continues:

"In fact, the Mappila attacks, Atjeh moord, and juramentado can all be regarded as regional variations on a more general theme, the creation of a Muslim heroic ideal in response to conflict with a non-Muslim power. This ideal represented the ideological expression of the militarised frontier society which Francois Ayard described in Kerala and Paul Wiltek analysed for early Ottoman society."

(Dale 1980 Page59)

The statement above precludes Dale to state the following:

"These attacks became especially prevalent in the late 19th century, representing, as they did in Atjeh and Kerala, an enraged frustration of Muslims with their military impotence and one of the few means of attack left to them as their Sultan gradually submitted to the Spanish."

(Dale 1980 Page 59)

Dale is therefore positing that the violent contradictions which were thrown up by European colonial expansion in South-East Asia from the 15th century onwards influenced the creation of a specific Asian Muslim warrior ideal.

The researcher would continue to show throughout this specific field of the text that Dale's position simply lacks the perspective offered by giving voice to the suppressed Islamic discourse. When allowed to speak, to constitute text, the experiences projected by the discourse teaches that it is not frontier society that forced Muslims to react via acts of "fruitless suicide" or martyrdom. Rather it is the discourse that constituted individuals to take action in a specific manner, the choice and method of response being constituted by the discourse but moreso the matrices of perception that viewed European assaults upon dar-al Islam within a discursively constituted worldview that insists that defence of the faith, din, must be effected to the point of death.

That the violent contradictions did ensure that Muslims in South East Asia resort to suicidal attacks out of growing military impotence is a statement born out of classic white causality given their specific worldview. Islamic discourse fostered and allowed various forms of responses to European expansionism, martyrdom was and is but one such constituted response. It was incumbent upon individual male Muslims to actually go through the mental mechanics of choosing the path of martyrdom as his specific response to the deprivations of the kafirs. It is these thought processes that precluded a male Muslim individual to embrace the path of martyrdom and the target of any researcher's enterprise who wants to give voice to suppressed voices, to unearth discourses.

The researcher's path was one which sought out texts that dealt with the muslims of the Philippines but in the exploration of texts sitting unused upon a library shelf, one realized the gargantuan task facing any researcher of the periphery who has accepted the challenge to create a textual continuum that gives voice to the silenced of the periphery. The researcher entered the field of texts stored for posterity on the library shelf devoted to the Philippines. From the outset it was most apparent that in the worldview that informs the choice of the texts to be acquired, Filipino Muslims are for all intents and purposes irrelevant. In a university library of the periphery the texts were singularly united and linked by their Orientalist worldview regardless of the political convictions of the authors or editors.

The "Marxist", liberal" and blatantly "conservative" authors or editors had one common position on Islam in the Philippines that is: its marginality to the mainstream colonial/neo colonial society. John Leddy Phelan in "The Hispanization of the Philippines" (Phelan 1967) presents but one variant of the re-current Islamophobic racist Western worldview as follows:

> "Islam's sway over the southern Philippines gave the Moros a political means of organizing successful resistance, for muslim cultural influence introduced the suprakinship unit of the state."

"Political-military authority was centralized sufficiently to organize effective resistance, but it never arrived at the point where the Spaniards could defeat and usurp it. What made the Moros unconquerable was the sound balance in their political-military organization between pre-muslim de-centralization and Muslim sponsored centralization."

(Phelan 1967 Page 143)

Phelan is trying his endeavour best to trivialize Islamic discourse to the point of irrelevance in the history of Filipino resistance to Spanish imperialism. The reason for this poor attempt at exorcising the Islamic demon from the white man's nightmares follows as Phelan bares his racist white worldview as he textualize thus:

"Judged by any objective standard, Spanish colonization in the Philippines was a remarkable episode in the global expansion of Europe. As an imperialist power the Spaniard's did their share in exploiting the resources of their Philippine colony, but in all fairness to that colonizing power it should be realized that Spain gave the Filipino's something in return. The pax hispanica created conditions of law and order throughout the maritime provinces of Luzon and the Bisayas, Spanish political institutions took deep root and Catholicism forged powerful new bonds of cultural unity."

(Phelan 1967 Page 161)

Phelan continues his textual white man's burden as follows:

"And finally Spain brought the Philippines into the orbit of Western civilization, from which they have not departed since the 16th century."

"As a direct consequence of Spanish colonization, the Filipino's are unique for being the only Oriental people profoundly and consistently influenced by Occidental culture for the last 4 centuries. In an Asia dominated by revolutionary and anti-western nationalism the consequences of this fact are a part of the world in which we live today."

(Phelan 1967 Page 161)

Phelan's worldview insists that Spanish colonialism saved the Philippines from Islamic domination or Islamization. In doing so the Philippines became situated in the "orbit of western civilization", He therefore praises the black skin white masks of the colonized Filipino for ultimately he sees the Philippines as the outpost of white neo-colonial domination in a hostile array of Oriental nations. The Philippines for him is then the beach head, the launching pad for the white man's excursions into a hostile South East Asia i.e. Vietnam. The zebras of the Philippines are the constituted objects of knowledge vital to the enterprise of white neo-colonial domination in South East Asia. Ever so assured in his white racist worldview Phelan is convinced that to be an Oriental with an Occidental worldview in the Orient is a condition in life vastly superior to that of being a Muslim living in the Orient. Yet another blatant example of the white man's ontological racism.

The journey through the texts continues as we textualize the text "Muslim Grievances and the Muslim Rebellion" (Noble 1987) by Lela Garner Noble. Noble's position on Muslim grievances in the Philippines is as follows:

> "Muslim grievances had been expressed in and derived from centuries of warfare against the Spaniards and their Filipino converts to Catholicism. Muslims in the southern Philippines intended to be neither conquered nor converted, and fought exhaustive battles to preserve freedom and Islam. They ultimately succumbed to American rule because the American's had superior weaponry and tactics, but they continued to protest incorporation into a centralized and in their perception Christian, Philippine government by whatever means they had at their disposal; running amok, organizing rebellion, presenting petitions or legislative proposals retreating into depression and/or isolation."

(Noble 1987 Page 419)

The "running amok" listed by Noble is in fact the martyrdom of the mujahid's and it is indicative of the way it is described by her "Running amok" is the discursive construct created by European colonialism to dismiss the relevance, the symbolic potency, the reverberation, the action of martyrdom creates in the perceptive worldview of both Muslim and Kuffir.

At the level of language the hegemonic European discourse constitutes an act of primitive and barbaric futility, the dying gasp of a beaten, defeated and conquered inferior people and culture. The perpetrator is a mindless emotion driven fanatic for he simply "ran amok". Within the Western hegemonic discourse since 1979 the martyr would be defined, summed up, conceptualised, held in co-ordinates of the perceptual matrix as a "fundamentalist". In effect the creation of pan optican matrices of perception that generate concepts that sum up actions of people of the periphery to and within the white man's discourse is at basic the constant attempts of the discourse to understand, to create causalities hence locate motivations for specific actions. Upon these structures of causalities the mechanism's charged with constituting individuals are erected, hence the unremitting clash of discourses within the person of the periphery seen in Noble's text that glaringly indicates the tensions of an intellectual position that is in antagonism to a specific stream of a ruling discourse yet it remains within the worldview that drives the discourse (Noble 1987A).

The second paper experienced by Lela Noble on the Muslim insurgency in the Philippines enabled the researcher the luxury of comparison. The first paper textualized was published in 1987 and the second in 1990; in both papers she refused to deal with the policies and strategies implemented by the Marcos and Aquino regimes to deal with the muslim guerrillas of the Moro National Liberation Front (MNLF). In both papers she deals at length with the factional infighting within the Muslim community and its inability militarily to liberate and hold territory in face of the military assaults of the Marcos and Aquino regimes. Noble betrays her worldview thus:

> "Obviously the MNLF is divided internally on its goals, and has not yet reached an accommodation with either Salamat's and Pundato's factions or with other Muslim leaders. Thus the Aquino government is likely to remain frustrated by Muslim factionalism. Yet arguably factionalism and the anarchy it produces should be considered an imperative for action rather than a reason for inaction. Continued delays in the development of an explicit Muslim agenda and the commitment to it of government attention and resources will only corroborate Muslim's suspicions that the Christian (and more specifically Catholic) government will not respond to their interests and needs until forced to do so by violence."

(Noble 1987)

What then Ms. Noble is "an explicit muslim agenda", in fact it is but another concept born out of the racist European worldview faced with the need to deal with a recalcitrant minority which has refused to be "whitened". There is then Ms. Noble in the United States of America a specific "Red man agenda", a "Nigger agenda" and a "Wet back agenda" and all these agendas involve decimation and subjection of its targets by any means necessary. That very method of genocide, the agenda of conquest and the constituting of zebra Filipino's by white racist discourse was implemented by the United States of America in its conquest and colonization of the Philippines and it is out of this discursive worldview she can speak of a "muslim agenda".

But what is this "muslim agenda" as implemented by successive regimes in the Philippines i.e. Marcos then Aquino? Leonard Davis in his text (Davis 1989) reports the "muslim agenda" at its lowest common denominator; its impact upon Muslims, Davis reports textually:

> "With a total population of 12 million, the island of Mindanao is the home of more than 5 million muslims and 1 million indigenous people. Poverty in the Muslim communities is as severe as in any other part of the archipelago. The Moro people in the Southern Philippines have nevertheless, a long tradition of resisting every attempt to subjugate them. For over 300 years they successfully repulsed all the armed expeditions of the Spanish colonialists and upheld their independence and culture. They also fought against the Japanese invaders in the Second World War."

> (Davis 1989 Page 44)

> "The Muslims in Mindanao have experienced untold pain and suffering during the last 2 decades, and the campaign of genocide was at its height during the Marcos era. The killings go on under Aquino, as Nur Misauri, chairman of the MNLF central committee, struggles to engage the government in a dialogue which could lead to the hope of a resolution to the problems."

> (Davis 1989 Pages 44-45)

"The genocidal campaign against the Bangsa Moro people started in March 1968 with the massacre of more than 70 muslim youths on the island of Corregidor, situated in Manila Bay."

"During the following decade, thousands upon thousands of muslims-most often women, children and the elderly people-and town after town were annihilated. The Ilago and the AFP, with money and weaponry supplied by the US, systematically murdered and ravaged the land throughout Muslim areas in Mindanao and Sulu archipelago. More than 100,000 people were slaughtered and 200,000 houses and Mosques were destroyed together with hundreds of Islamic schools, and vast plantations."

"In all the massacres, men were beheaded, pregnant women were mutilated and disembowelled, and children's ears were cut off. Ear cutting became a ritual on the part of both the AFP and the Ilaga. At certain times for every pair of Moro ears handed in, there was a government reward."

(Davis 1989 Page 45)

The two accounts by Lela Noble and one by RJ May (May 1985) on the "muslim insurgency" no mention is made of the "final solution" adopted by successive Philippine governments. In its focus, its methodology, its symbolism, the" final solution" of the "muslim agenda" in the Philippines is the product of European colonialism/neo-colonialism and the racist discourse/worldview that drives it, that replicates it across linear time.

The ear cutting is not unique for it was practised with mind numbing barbarity by the racist Belgian colonizer in the Congo Basin of Africa, likewise in the "Indian agenda" of the white man's conquest of the Native Americans, they also mutilated the bodies of Indians the most famous of the mutilations being scalp hunting. The pedigree runs through and with the worldview for in Vietnam the mutilation of the Viet Cong and the North Vietnamese Army regulars was practised by American troops. Today it continues in Bosnia Herzegovina. What other lessons were afforded the researcher on this journey through the textualisings of the Muslim reactions to their minority status in a perceptually hostile environment.

The primary lesson must be repeated and this is the silenced voice of the discourse besieged. The texts available simply were not interested in giving voice to the persons locked in the discursive contradictions. The thought processes that motivated the choice of action taken and the perceptive structures of the worldview that created the range of choices of action all remain lost for the human who initiated action is either dead or locked in his internal dialogue. At best the choices remain locked within the mental process of reflection, choice and action for there is no conviction to give voice to these thought processes, to challenge the human owners of these processes, to articulate them, to create texts upon and around them.

The martyrdom of the human vindicates the worldview of the discourse in which he situated himself and voices are afforded the martyrs within the Islamic discourse. But to the non-Islamic discourses the alternatives are to embrace the Islamic discourse and find and "listen" to the voices of martyrdom thereby transporting those voices across the discursive zone of attrition into the non-Islamic discourse. Or to do what has been done repeatedly within the fields of European racist discourse by "listening" to the voices through matrices of perception that distort the voice to render it audible to the worldview of the listener. The "ears" of the listener are constituted objects of knowledge, the products of hegemonic racist discourse. These "ears" are then tone deaf to all other sounds, voices save and except those emanating from its discursive creator." Voices" that cross the discursive frontier can only then be "heard" via mechanism that render them audible, perceptible to the listener.

All perceptions grounded in discourse/worldview can only perceive what is constitutable by its worldview/discourse. What cannot be constituted is non-existant, a hallucination, a sophism, the agnostic. The end result is, among streams of other things, enterprises of the mental workers of the periphery unable and unwilling to cross the wasteland of the zone of discursive attrition to give voice to alternate worldviews, to open tunnels that span the discursive war zone that are necessary to understanding, to reconciliation, to decolonization, to destruction of the fractured, ambivalent, schizophrenic personages that constantly feed and replicate the racist frankenstein monsters that tear at our beings in the periphery,denying us wholeness.

We as the children of Sisyphus are doomed in every moment of our existence to replicate the discursive structures that constitute our dependence of worldview. The children of Sisyphus are doomed to replicate the barbarity of the white racist colonial system with the white man now one stage removed from the logistics of barbarity. The children of Sisyphus have learnt all too well at the foot, nay underneath the foot of the master race and we are now secure in our convictions that to replicate self-immolation and racist hatred is our chosen purpose in life. By replicating the racist discourse of the white man we constantly seek to prove to him our deservedness, our suitability to join his dominant, hegemonic worldview.

The ultimate price we are willing to pay for entry to this club, and do pay on a daily basis is self hatred and deprecation manifested through various actions, the most despicable being black on black racism to the point of genocide that would make Hitler, Himmler and Goebbels rub their master race hands in glee for the "final solution" is now more than ever on the agenda with the master race no longer the perpetrator but now the philanthropist, the humanist. Millions of victims of white racism since 1492 cry out in shame at the actions of these zebras of the periphery.

The secondary lessons culled from the texts are as follows: The phase of guerrilla warfare since 1968 launched by the Muslims of the Philippines was facilitated by the support of members of the Ummah, specifically Muammar Gaddafi of Lybia and Tun Mustapha of Sabah. The MNLF in the face of a relentless campaign of genocide waged against muslims in the Philippines have had to create space for the guerrilla insurgency by lobbying the oil rich muslims of the ummah to apply pressure to oil dependent Philippine governments to negotiate a peaceful settlement to the insurgency. In the absence of the support of the ummah the insurgency in the Philippines would have ground to a halt many years past for both the lack of the materials of war and the failure to create spaces that give temporary reprieves from the relentless attacks of the military.

The eclipsing of the insurgency of the MNLF by the New People's Army (NPA) has now allowed the MNLF to create spaces of stalemate as the NPA has been now targeted as the primary insurgency for obvious reasons, but the fact that the NPA has an effective operational presence on the island of Mindanao indicates the cross fertilization that occurred between the MNLF and the NPA. The initial insurgency of the MNLF in the late 1960's, the response of the military and the flow of material to Mindanao created the perceptual and objective conditions that gave birth to the NPA in Mindanao.

Finally the texts of the Philippines yielded instances again of the transcendent role of racism in the white man's worldview. The modus operandi of conquest, of colonial domination, of pacification, spanning the arrival of the

Spanish in the 16th century to the Americans in the 19th century regardless of mode of production, historical epoch or technological base was driven by, defined and implemented through the perspectives constituted by a racist, supremacist worldview. The Spanish attacks upon the Muslims were expected given their unrelenting hatred of Muslims as their overlords in Spain. But the repeated attacks upon the Negritos of the mountain regions of Luzon and their use of converted Filipino's to wage war upon the black hill people marked the genesis of black on black racism in the Philippines. For the war against the Negritos was informed by the fact that they are non-white recalcitrant heathens.

The American conquest of the Philippines was framed and expressed in blatantly racist language; it was the language of conquest. General Shafter's words:

> "It may be necessary to kill half of the Filipinos in order that the remaining half of the population may be advanced to a higher plane of life than their present semi-barbarous state affords."

> (Francisco 1987 Page 11)

Extracts from a letter written by a U.S. serviceman in the Philippines:

> "On Thursday, March 29 (19.00)…18 of my company killed 75 nigger bowmen and 10 of the nigger gunners…When we find one who is not dead, we have bayonets…"

> (Francisco 1987 Page 13)

General (Howling) Jake Smith speaks:

> "Kill and burn, kill and burn, the more you kill and the more you burn, the more you please me."

> (Francisco 1987 Page 17)

The words are not unique, the perceptions that motivates the action are not new and the list of brutality and genocide perceptually motivated by white racism insists that racism in the white man's worldview is ontologically centred and a major component, even the lynchpin of his worldview. The constituted Filipino, the black skinned white masked, oriental trapped in an occidental worldview, the zebra, the filo-Saxon never failed to replicate the phantoms of their masters' racist worldview. The zebras of the dominant mainstream neo-colonial worldview must replicate the others, the back boards upon which to rebound their schizophrenic/neurotic images of being.

In the Philippines the discourse constituted others who are demographic minorities-the black clans of the mountains who refused to accept the white man's catholic worldview, the Muslims of the South who refused to accept the white man's worldview full stop. And the Chinese immigrant community which is the other's other in effect they became the niggers/Hymie of the Philippines replete with Chinatown and pogroms. The quintessential example of mainstream Filipino discourse is Cory Aquino who during her tenure as President of the Republic never failed to perpetuate the programs dictated by her worldview. Aquino therefore continued Marcos' wars against the Muslims, the NPA and the forcible seizure of lands controlled by the Negritos thereby creating reserves in the tradition of the United States of America and its "Indian agenda". Marcos was therefore a minor hiccup in the hegemony of the neo-colonial racist worldview of the Phillippines, the rest is a given for the worldview can only constitute the long list of brutalities and genocide it inherited from its creators.

In ending this textual journey through the texts that deal with the realities of the Philippines the researcher ends with a Muslim's perception of this said reality.M.Ali Kettani speaks:

> "In the 16th century, the islands which make up today the Philippines were in an advanced state of Islamization.Three muslim states extended their influence on these islands; the Sulu Muslim state including Sulu, Basilan, Palawan, Negros, Panay, Mindoro and Iloco in the north of Luzon islands; the Maguindanao muslim state, including the entire island of Mindanao; and the Muslim state of Manilad (today's Manila) including the Center of Luzon."

> "The first victim of this colonial attack was the Muslim state of Manilad.But muslim resistance organized itself in the south of the islands of Palawan, Sulu and Mindanao.These islands became part of a united independent muslim state of the Sulu's. Spain could

never conquer this state in spite of continuous warfare, and had to recognize its independent existence."

"The Americans succeeded in conquering the Spanish colony in 1899,but the Muslim state of Sulu resisted. It fell to the American arms in 1914 after a long and heroic struggle."

"On March 11 1915,the Muslim king (Sultan) was forced to abdicate...."

"It was only in April 1940 that the Americans abolished the Sultanate of Sulu and incorporated Bangsa Moro in the Philippines."

(Kettani 1986 Page 135)

"Thus Bangsa Moro is a Muslim land whose population follows the Shafii school. It was colonized by the Philippines in 1940 and has remained so ever since. After independence from the US, the indigenous populations of the northern islands which had been forcibly converted to Catholicism by Spain, followed up the same policy of genocide against the muslims which they had inherited from the Spanish colonial establishment and which had been encouraged and supported by the US."

(Kettani 1986 Pages 135-136)

"The Catholic Church remained the moving power behind the brutal de-Islamization and Christianisation of the south in the same way it had been the moving power behind the Spanish Inquisition."

(Kettani 1986 Page 136)

The clash of the worldviews that constituted the texts presented here becomes evident when Kettani's text is inserted. His perspectives stand in the stark glaring opposition to the texts of non-muslims experienced by the researcher. He insists that Bangsa Moro fought to maintain its distinct identity from the clutches of Spanish and American colonialism. By dint of this Bangsa Moro does not form part of the entity termed the Philippines for that is conquered, colonized, christianised territory-dar ul Harb-, the abode of Kuffirs, the domain of Jahiliyya. Bangsa Moro-dar al Islam-was annexed to the Philippines by the Americans and the neo-colonial Catholic Filipino elite has forcibly colonized Bangsa Moro since 1940.

For Kettani and the worldview he articulates there can be but one strategy, one option, one choice left to muslims of Bangsa Moro-Jihad-, war in defence of the faith (din), tradition, war in defence of dar ul Islam therefore the guerrilla insurgency is ordained by Islam and martyrdom the choice of action for muslims who so make the decision to adopt it as their ultimate and final test of their submission to the will of Allah. For him the only solution to the present impasse would be de-coupling Bangsa Moro from the Philippines. The MNLF has repeatedly insisted that its minimum bargaining position is autonomy for geographic areas, which have Muslims as the majority of the population. The filo-Saxons have repeatedly made treaties recognizing this right to Muslim self-determination and have repeatedly failed to implement the terms of these treaties.

The neo-colonial worldview of the hegemonic zebras cannot tolerate alienation of sections of their sacrosanct "nation state" to the control of alternate worldviews. Rather than willingly allow the Muslims to go in peace, the zebras would rather destroy the sum of the wholes to retain a fraction of the whole. The most potent example of this is Serbia and the non-Serb fractions of what was once Yugoslavia. Again the researcher can only posit that the fetish of hegemony over space, over geography, over parts of mother earth and the people and other sentient beings found therein springs from the specificities of the white man's ontology of being. For the desire to dominate, to hold, to possess, to control, to own mother earth and all her sentient beings is an overwhelming desire uniquely, relentlessly part of the history of the white man especially since that fateful day in 1492. To understand this white phenomenon we focus at the level of desire and its interaction with discourse. But exploration of this is outside the scope of this present enterprise.

The researchers' journey through and with the textualising of texts ends with the textual gaze into the most potent minority worldview within Islamic discourse i.e. Shi'i Islamic discourse and the Islamic Revolution of Iran in 1979. The journey would be textual and the first text deconstructed is "The Spirit of Allah, Khomeini and the Islamic Revolution" by Amir Taheri (Taheri 1987). He states:

"Once Khomeini had seized control of Iran, my journalistic curiosity concerning his life and thoughts immediately became a moral necessity. I had to get to know this almost total stranger who had captured the imagination of my compatriots with his discourse and who was now changing beyond recognition the Iran I had grown to love above everything else."

(Taheri 1987 Page 16)

The inevitable attraction, the beckoning of the text to the researcher was Taheri's statement on the power of Khomeini's discourse. The desire to experience the text heightened with his insistence on the centrality of Khomeini and his discourse in the creation of the Islamic Revolution 1979. Taheri states:

"During the past 7 years many attempts have been made to minimize the role of Khomeini in conceiving and then realizing his design for an Islamic Revolution and an Islamic state."

"The success of the Imam in leading a religious revolution to victory in the 20th century is a rare achievement. But his success in creating the world's first and only theocratic state since the fall of the Dalai Lama in Tibet is surely unique. The Imam's revolution is the only example of a successful Muslim revolt against a western or western style system of government."

(Taheri 1987 Page 19)

Taheri sums up the ultimate significance of the Islamic Revolution 1979 for those of us of the periphery for it indicated by its praxis the ability of Islamic discourse to reverse the hegemony enjoyed by the secularising/modernizing discourse of the Iranian zebras summed up in the person of Shah Reza Pahlavi.

The researcher's quest is then to understand the discursive structures, which drove the Islamic discourse of Iran to hegemony, specifically the re-definition of these structures, which sprang from the praxis of Ruhollah Khomeini. Firstly we experience instances from his texts:

"The world is but a passage, it is not a world in which we ought to live. This (world) is but a way; it is the Narrow Path.... What is called Life in this world is not life but death. True life is that offered only in the hereafter...We are here in this low, earthly life, because of our ignorance consider these duties to be onerous; but these are verily, the best example of the Almighty's generosity (towards us).... No one becomes a true human being without first crossing the narrow path."

Ayatollah Khomeini in an address commemorating the 7th day of his son's Mostafa's death in Najaf Iraq.

(Taheri 1987 Page 37)

"Perdition begins with but a small step, a tiny step that can be dismissed as insignificant. Man moves towards Hell step by step. All those who were lost did not become corrupt all of a sudden with a giant leap as it were. They began with tiny insignificant steps and were soon beyond salvation. There is a devil in every man, corrupting him little by little."

(Taheri 1987 Page 67)

The following, are two poems of Khomeini, which flow, in discursive continuity with the texts above:

"It's spring and there is blossom on the almond tree. The bride of the garden is, verily the almond tree. A sight that gives comfort to all tired eyes, filling with joy the hearts of widows and orphans. To the sick man, to the dying it gives hope of cure a message from the creator is this almond tree. It tells you that; beauty and life are created from the ugly earth that wore the death mask of winter. Carefree and joyful, flock to the garden young and old foolishly taking as eternal the blossoms of the tree. And yet suddenly the sky darkens with a thunderous cloud. Rain shakes the almond tree, scattering its blossoms. The bride of the garden stands naked and trembling, like an old beggar woman chased off a street. A moments oblivion, the ingratitude of one moment leads to a terrible lesson for those who forget God. "Hindi", knowing all this, remembers at every breath, not the beauty of the blossoms but he who made them."

(Taheri 1987 Page 324)

"I know not in which book I read the story of Tamarlane's exploits. He who put young and old to the sword. he who ignored the commands of the Lord. At night he was struck by insomnia crying aloud and writhing with pain. Doctors who came to offer him a cure saw the wound of a sword around his neck strangling him. That's the revenge of God. So as the Tatar pierced the roof with his cries, the Angel of Revenge chuckled noiselessly. There is one who lays the mighty low. There is he who chops the guilty into pieces. To him is devoted "Hindi" and to no other one."

(Taheri 1987 Page 325)

The textual selections from the textualisings of Khomeini listed above indicate the deep esoteric, the Shi'i esoteric bedrock upon which Khomeini's worldview was founded. These selections flow out of the streams of Islamic esoterica presented as the first textual survey of the researcher in the first steps of his journey of understanding. To his death Khomeini lived the lifestyle of a Sufi mystic austere and disciplined in his praxis to the point where the outer manifestations were the result of an inner conviction, austerity and discipline.

In the post 1979 realities of Iran, the Ayatollah Khomeini's lifestyle, his personal praxis never wavered, nor changed to suit the demands of political power. In fact the obverse was the rule as the political culture was re-structured to fit into his very private and secluded world of his praxis. For Khomeini submission to God was paramount in his praxis and this submission was total and all encompassing. Thus he says:

"The Imam (Ali) teaches that, as Allah is aware, we have not risen in order to secure positions of authority and become a government. We have no objective other than saving the oppressed from their oppressors. All that made me accept the rulership of the community is Almighty God's strict instruction that the clergy should not remain silent in the face of greed and oppressive profiteering and

the soul-crushing hunger of the downtrodden." Ayatollah
Khomeini in Valayat-e-Faqih

(Taheri 1987 Page 171)

"The fire is rising out of the Temples of Fire in Persia and fed by the
followers of Zarathustra and Mazdak must be extinguished, or else
the fire-worshipping rabble shall lead you back to the heathen practises of Magus." Kasaf al Asrar

(Taheri 1987 Page 105)

Khomeini saw the Shah Reza Pahlavi as the epitome of the movement to
return Iran to the era of Jahiliyyah. For Khomeini to create Iran in the image
and likeness of the West was tantamount to a declaration of war upon dar al
Islam by Shah Reza Pahlavi. How was Khomeini then to wage this war against
the discourse of secularisation/modernization? Khomeini says:

"Those who oppose the mullahs oppose Islam itself, eliminate the
mullahs and Islam shall disappear for 50 years. It is only the mullahs
who can bring the people into the streets and make them die for
Islam-begging to have their blood shed for Islam."

(Taheri 1987 Page 51)

"Islam was dead or dying for nearly 14 centuries; we have revived it
with the blood of our youth...We shall soon liberate Jerusalem and
pray there."

(Taheri 1987 Page 247)

Both textual instances listed embrace two discursive constructs of
Khomeini's praxis of revolution which are (a) the primacy of the mullah as
leader of the ummah or the community of believers and (b) primacy of martyrdom as the means of confrontation with the enemies of Islam.

Khomeini destroyed the uneasy truce that existed between the mullahs and
the ruling political elites of the day in Iran by now insisting that the mullah
must now control the political structures of Islamic society. But he went fur-

ther by positing himself as the Islamic alternative to the Shah by describing himself as the Imam. The re-definition of himself as the Imam allowed, enabled visualizations, perceptions of the dualist struggle between good/evil, Islam/Jahiliyya in the persons of Shah/Imam, Reza Pahlavi/Khomeini. This dualist construct threw up texts as follows:

> "The day the Imam returns no one will tell lies anymore, no one will lock the door of his house; people will become brothers, sharing the bread of their joys together in justice and in sincerity. There will no longer be any queues; queues of bread and meat, queues of kerosene and petrol, queues of cinemas and buses, queues of tax payments, queues of snake poison shall all disappear. And the dawn of awakening and the spring of freedom shall smile upon us. The Imam must return...so that right can sit on its throne, so that evil, treachery and hatred are eliminated from the face of time. When the Imam returns, Iran-this broken, wounded mother will forever be liberated from the shackles of tyranny and ignorance and the chains of plunder, torture and prison." The Day the Imam Returns by Taha Hejazi.

> (Taheri 1987 Page 227)

In the struggle of the dualities in contradiction it was inevitable that the mullah would upon seizing power through the hegemony of Islamic discourse move to create structures to ensure their hegemony as the new political elite. The discursive structure that constituted the military arm of the struggle to supplant the ruling hegemonic discourse of the day was martyrdom.

Khomeini drew upon the discursive stream of martyrdom presented previously in this text and the specific perceptions of martyrdom in Shi'i discourse embraced to create a discourse of martyrdom of relevance to Iran in 1979. He drew upon the perceptions of martyrdom unique to Shi'i Islamic discourse an example of which is:

> "The sky becomes black, floods of tears are unleashed. Hussein arrives in Karbala to sacrifice himself to Allah. This is the story of Ashura. Hear this tale of great sorrow and shed tears for the King of Martyrs who shall take you to paradise." Popular mourning poem from the Ta'azieh Passion Plays.

> (Taheri 1987 Page 133)

To constitute the object of knowledge of the Islamic Revolution who produced texts as such:

> "How poor, how miserable, how ignorant was I in all the 14 years of my wretched life that was passed in the ignorance of Allah. The Imam gave light to my eyes.... How sweet, sweet, sweet is death-this blessing of Allah to those who are favoured."

> "What a joy to fight alongside friends, and to die alongside friends on the road to paradise."

> (Taheri 1987 Page 286)

Via the circular dance of dualities in contradiction Khomeini developed the specific discursive structure of martyrdom in the service of Islam under the leadership of the Imam for the preservation of Islam.

This was a discursive creation entirely the creation of Khomeini and it effectively popularized, even democratised martyrdom as no longer the preserve of specific heroic personalities of Shi'i Islamic discourse as Hussein. Khomeini expounded the discursive structure of martyrdom ensuring its reverberation and reverie in the perceptions of his listeners by utilizing the discursive Shi'i crowbar of discourse termed rowzeh. Rowzeh is a specific technique of the vocal delivery of discourse, which motivates specific actions of the listener by presenting a continuum of analogies on the martyrdom of Hussein and the tragedy of Karbala. Khomeini used rowzeh in his discourse to link the action of martyrdom to the perceptions of his listeners by insisting that martyrdom was now the duty of all Muslims in the struggle of good vs evil.

The effectiveness of the discursive structure in constituting martyrs is demonstrated by the thousands of graves of the martyrs, which threaten to engulf the geography of Tehran. Instances of the slogans used in the struggle against the Shah indicate the specificities of Khomeini's discourse of revolution. Instances chosen are as follows:

> "Allah is the Greatest, Khomeini is the leader."
> "Allah, Qur'an, Khomeini."
> "Death to the Shah."

"The American Shah must be put to death."
"The only way to salvation is Faith, Holy War and Martyrdom."

(Taheri 1987 Page 286)

What then were the other discursive structures that empowered Khomeini within his worldview to counter the cut and thrust of the daily struggles for hegemony between contending worldviews?

The structures identified, the perceptions they enabled and the actions, which sprang from these perceptions, are summarized as follows:

(a) Takfir (anathema) and hijra (withdrawal). An inward manifestation of the call to enjoin what is good and forbid what is evil, applied whenever the Shi'i mullahs were as a cohesive group or individually unable to overcome the forces of opposition to Islam in Iran. Ruhollah Khomeini was the Ayatollah to publicly call for the offensive against the Shah thereby moving takfir and hijra from an inward to outward manifestation of the Muslim.

(b)Ketman teaches the pursuit of two contradictory objectives simultaneously, thereby establishing the practitioner to be perceived in contradictory manners, which creates perceptual space in which to work, through dissimulation.

(c) Khodeh teaches use of deception to the enemies of Islam to ensure that one's true position remains untouched/unreachable through the enemy's mis-understanding/misjudgement of the Muslim's position.

(d)Tanfih teaches the neutralizing of a Muslim's potential rivals or enemies.

(e) Taqieh teaches the use of blatant lies and other forms of deception to enable victory over the enemies of Islam in a hostile environment. Khomeini successfully planned, developed and utilised discourses of deception utilising the discursive structures outlined above thereby becoming to all his audiences exactly what they perceived via their respective worldviews whilst Khomeini's worldview remained hidden to be revealed as the dictates of power demanded.

Shi'i Islamic discourse enabled Khomeini to perceive the streams of hege-monic discourse with which Islamic discourse was locked in battle and devise specific discourses to address these streams thereby neutralizing them as power relations dictated. The best examples of this were the manner in which the relations with the USA were handled and relations with the left wing agglomerations of Iran. Under the guidance of Khomeini Islamic discourse moved all challenges in its path primarily because the challenge of alternate discourses were weak and ineffective.

It is in fact indicative that the most effective challenge to date to the rule of the mullahs came from within the discourse by the Mujahideen-e-Khalq whose contradiction is with the hegemony of the mullah rather than with the hegemony of Islamic discourse.

Textual instances from the minds of the martyrs of the Mujahideen-e-Khalq would indicate the powerful reverberations that the discursive structures trigger in the perceptions of the constituted object of knowledge through the window of martyrdom. Reverberations exclude the centrality of the Imam for in the perceptions of the Mujahideen-e-Khalq the martyr's responsibility to the Ummah, to Islam is not mediated through the Imam. The worldview of the Mujahideen-e-Khalq made violent confrontation with the hegemony of the mullah inevitable aptly demonstrated in the widely variant worldviews expressed through both bodies of text. Instances of the texts are as follows;

SHAHADAT 1976

On this dawn of blood my message to you is shahadat

The mujahid guerrilla knows not defeat I'm a shaheed

Blessed for me is shahadat dawn is stretching evil withdrawing

Rage is rising to become God's hand and bursts from the sleeve of Mujahideen

Shahadat is a blessing Shahadat is liberation it's the path to a world knit in divine integration

I've staked my life on God's command I'm liberated from all prisons

But with the people share their imprisonment

Lo, is bursting from the Mujahideen's gun Shahadat! Shahadat!

A message from Quran coming from God to favour the oppressed and the weak

God has urged Muslims with the message the acme of life's line is shahadat

Blazed in the night of oppression like a star I heed this message I'm a Muslim

So long as there is oppression and injustice I'm a shaheed! I'm a shaheed!

(Irfani 1983 Page 255)

THE SONG OF BLOOD 1971-72
When our blood began flowing on the path of truth the seeds of
revolution quickened with life The spark of people's vengeance set
fire to the straw house of the people's enemy
On the revolution's sky a star is born the way for the final battle has
been opened
Through his worldview and the Mujahid's machine gun arise and
commit yourself truly, with the resoluteness of blood and steel
Arise, for the Hand of God will burst out from the people's sleeve
Arise! Arise! The time of revolution is being raised by the
Mujahideen.

(Irfani 1983 Page 255)

Instances of the worldviews of Khomeini and the Mujahideen-e-Khalq
when juxtaposed, when offered up as pieces of a discursive jigsaw puzzle have
revealed the deep underlying basis of the violent contradiction that developed
between them. The Mujahideen worldview is clearly the outcome of the move
to blend western leftist worldviews with Islamic discourse in Iran. The worldview attempts a marriage of Che and Mao with Islamic discourse. For without
retention of Islamic credentials the western leftist worldview in Iran is simply
irrelevant.

Khomeini's position on this discursive mulatto was self-evident for when
the Mujahideen moved militarily against the hegemony of the mullah's the
ensuing battle was brutal and the Islamic rules of war were simply suspended.
His worldview could not embrace the Mujahideen for in its simplicity the
analogy is profound that is the analogy of the almond tree. He is not lured into
the trap of being enthralled by the beauty of its blossoms thereby forgetting he
who created the almond tree.

In this journey through the textual instances of the Islamic discourse,
specifically seeking instances of the discourse in geographic areas where Islam
is in a minority position, the researcher has traced the existence of specific discursive structures, which enable adherents of the discourse to construct specific matrices of perception, which respond to their minority position. These
matrices of perception are welded to schemata of possible action options
available to the Muslim, as determined by his worldview. The lesson of this
journey is the fact that Muslims in a minority position upon perceiving that

the survival of Islam is threatened have responded via modes of action, which follow the courses of the worldview regardless of whatever historical epoch they may find themselves in. The ummah in a minority position would always produce a range of actions empowered by the discourse.

What all non-muslims should note and internalise within their worldview is that when the ummah perceives that its existence is up for grabs, the recourse to jihad, expressed in the state of martyrdom is a given valid and discursively constituted course of action which would always be embraced by members of the Ummah. The action of the Jamaat al Muslimeen on the afternoon of July 27th 1990 was therefore within the Islamic discourse a perfectly valid action mandated by the discourse in the face of a perceived threat of genocide against the Ummah. The military strike against the policing agencies of the state by the Jamaat al Muslimeen stands grounded in the history of Islamic discourse and its contradiction with kaffirs.

The textual journeys, which preceded this clearly shows that the Jamaat al Muslimeen drew upon the streams of, the discourse in devising the course of action launched on July 27th 1990. The military strike was in no way the actions of a lunatic fringe for in their worldview and discursive realities the action is validated, sanctioned and has been replicated through the history of the discourse since that fateful day of battle between Islam and Jahiliyya in Arabia in the era of the Prophet. And in the din and clatter of history the words of the Imam continue to resonate, to reverberate, to evoke reverie in the matrices of perception of Muslims of the post Islamic Revolution 1979 era. A textual instance of these words is as follows:

> "Brothers, do not sit at home so that they (the enemy) attack. Move onto the offensive and be sure that they shall retreat...This was what happened in Iran and Iran's power was far greater than most of the other countries.... Do not content yourself with teaching the people the rules of prayer and fasting. The rules of Islam are not limited to these.... Why don't you recite the sura of qital? Why should you always recite the suras of mercy? There are ills that cannot be cured except through burning. The corrupt in every society should be liquidated.... The Quran teaches us to treat as brothers only those who are Muslims and believe in Allah. (It) teaches us to

treat those who are not thus differently, teaches us to hit them, throw them in gaol and kill them...."

(Taheri 1987 Page 305)

The journey continues and the researcher pauses to textualise two sign-posts on the path to clarity. The Soviet invasion of Afghanistan, the continued war of attrition against the muslims of the Philippines, the anti-muslim pogroms of India and in the decade of the 1990's the genocide of Bosnia have continued to etch in the perceptions of minority muslims the world over the tenuous positions they are trapped within dar al Harb.

Graphic sights of holocaust in Bosnia continue to assault the perceptions of minority muslims the world over and the ummah has responded with the creation of a discursive concept that grapples with the reality of a perceived strategy of genocide waged against muslims the world over. The concept of Muslimicide (See Echo of Islam No.109/110 July/August 1993) and the discursive structures that embrace it insist that there is a master plan by the west to eliminate Islamic minorities wherever they constitute threats to the hegemony of the western worldview. The response to Muslimicide by the ummah must be, can only be framed within the discursive structures of martyrdom by both the Muslims faced with Muslimicide and the international Ummah. In response to Muslimicide in Bosnia the discourse has re-tooled its mechanism's towards the constituting of objects of knowledge and the texts have flowed in the streams of perceptive grappling with the realities of Bosnia. Instances of one text are as follows:

"My childhood came to an abrupt end, when the war began.
All of a sudden I had to be my own father...my own mother...
It was a precocious coming of age.
I left my city, my father, my mother, my brother, defending the city...
I left all my toys behind...and I was taken on the roads punctuated by checkpoints
I was taken to cities whose languages I did not know, nor wished to know...
I still speak my own language, even to those who don't understand it...

I refuse to become a gypsy, speaking the languages of the world...
(in perpetual Diaspora, entertaining the street crowds in the four
corners of the world in order to survive....)
I speak my own language and soon I am going to learn the language
of my brother a language our enemies fear the most, the language of
the gun...."
From "Give My Heart to Bosnia" by H.Tehrani

(Echo of Islam No. 109/110 July/August 1993)

The other signpost that forced a pause in the enterprise of the researcher is
the appearance of texts from within hegemonic western academia, which now
articulate discourse, a worldview that offers liberation from the hegemonic
worldview of the white man. Moreso, it is but a stream of a flowing river of
worldviews of the periphery that are now challenging the hegemony of the
white man's discourse.

The specific text is titled: "The Political significance for Muslims of the
Islamic Revolution in Iran" by Salim Mansur (Echo of Islam No.109/110
July/August 1993), University of Western Ontario. Instances of Mansur's text
would indicate this new discourse/worldview that is emerging in the West on
Islam.Mansur states:

> "The challenges of the Islamic revolution to the West have very little
> to do with military-ideological-economic confrontation. Instead
> the Islamic revolution demands of the west space for itself, within
> its own historical boundaries, to reconstruct and reinvent Muslim
> history without intervention."

> "It is in this perspective the militancy of the Islamic revolution
> unfolding in the 20th century did not represent a nostalgic rever-
> sion to the past, but a rejoining of history disconnected by the colo-
> nial interlude."

> "The Islamic worldview of the Iranian revolution sets it apart from
> all other revolutions in the 20th century."

"In affirming the Islamic worldview, the Islamic Republic of Iran emerged as a counterpoint to the west and its hegemonic influence within the muslim world."

"While modernity, as Foucault pointed out, is "often characterized in terms of consciousness of the discontinuity of time" of a break with tradition, the Islamic Revolution with it's emphasis on tradition may be described as a significant example of "counter-modernity" in contemporary history."

(Mansur 1993)

It is therefore fitting to end this specific segment of the researchers journey of discovery with the perception that confirms the realization that ideas simply don't fall from the sky.

The discursive streams flow through the perceptions and actions of its adherents and no constituted object of discourse stands alone for even Robinson Crusoe brought with him his worldview to the island of his exile for without it he could not have constituted his man Friday. Likewise people of the periphery who have tirelessly journeyed through the textual instances of western academic discourse are now creating a conjuncture within the discourse. A conjuncture pregnant with the birth of a new product of discursive evolution, which is destined to be the alternate discourse of the peoples of the periphery, trapped within Western academic discourse. This alternate worldview would momentarily escalate its desire and battle for hegemony for its day has come after that too long interlude, that interregnum since 1492.

For those of us who have laboured in the fields of futility seeking the elusive holy grail it is a move for hegemony too long in coming for the peoples of the periphery have paid dearly for our subjection. Our discursive freedom would be bought with the blood of the martyrs from the native peoples of Guanahani in 1493 to the people of Haiti in 1994. At times one wonders if the price of freedom invalidates the state of discursive hegemony, one simply wonders.

"PRANCING THEY COME"
SEE THEM PRANCING
THEY COME NEIGHING,
THEY COME A HORSE NATION
SEE THEM PRANCING
THEY COME NEIGHING,
THEY COME.

(Brown 1976 Pg 99)

Chapter 2

ISLAMIC DISCOURSE: SPECIFICITIES

INTRODUCTION

The text that follows deals primarily with streams of discursivities that flow and merge to constitute Islamic discourse and instances of each discursivity chosen are presented via the exegesis of specific texts of the authors chosen. Given the events of 11 September 2001 in New York an additional text of Sayyed Mawdudi and the letter of one of the alleged Shahids of 11 September 2001 were included for deconstruction. The reader must be aware of the reality that the backbone of this text was written in an attempt to understand the Jihad waged by the Jamaat al Muslimeen in the form of an attempted coup d'etat against the kuffir state of Trinidad and Tobago, West Indies on July 27th 1990.The attack on the World Trade Center, New York was not precluded by the attempted coup d'etat of 1990 in Trinidad and the question now arises of the genesis of these actions in Islamic discourse. This is a most relevant debate for the Ummah Wasat that finds itself a minority in the West. The raging debate of Jihad in the West especially as it impacts upon da'wa and its effectiveness has been a raging debate within the Ummah of Trinidad and Tobago since July 27th 1990 and such is the turn now of the Ummah in the US.

The streams of discursivities selected are (a) Sufi Mysticism or esoteric Islamic discourse, (b) Sunni militant Islam, (c) Shi'i militant Islam, (d) Islam in a minority position/Islam in a non-Islamic nation state. In no way am I going to present an historical account of streams of discourse. What I intend to do is to present via the texts reviewed the discursive structures that bolster these streams of discourse and begin the mapping of the flow of these streams of discourse into the Jamaat al Muslimeen at the conjuncture of July 27th 1990. The final outcome of this exercise would be a cartographic discursive expression of the streams of discourse that flowed into that specifically and spatially unique worldview within Islamic discourse that constituted the action taken on July 27th 1990.

Sufi Mysticism or esoteric Islamic discourse was deliberately chosen because of the long-standing antagonism between the exoteric and esoteric stream of Islamic discourse. While both insist that Islam is an ortho-praxis that culminates in salvation of the Muslim. For the Sufi mystic salvation specifically deals with the state/mode of existence after physical death in which the believer/Muslim evades the judgment of Allah by existing eternally in Paradise.

The Holy Quran states as follows:

> "God hath promised to believers, Men and Women,
> Gardens under which rivers flow, To dwell therein, And beautiful
> mansions, In Gardens of everlasting bliss. But the greatest bliss is
> the good pleasure of God; that is the supreme felicity."

> Sura ix-72

The Sufi mystics insist that there is an esoteric meaning that parallels, that flanks the exoteric meaning of the Holy Quran. And the evidence for this is found in the specific Arabic structures used in the text of the Holy Quran. The language of revelation via the written text, the basis of Islamic discourse is then the driving force of Sufi mysticism. God's revelation to humans is always expressed via language and text and even when the Sufi retreats into the world of experiential knowledge based on meditation, self-reflection, the language of revelation can never be discarded. For it is only by immersion within the text of revelation that oneness with God is achieved. The text of revelation is then the foundation of Islamic discourse in both its esoteric and exoteric streams.

Seyyed Hossein Nasr in the works: "Islamic Life and Thought", 1981 and "Sufi Essays" 1972 would be reviewed as the principal author in this section on Sufi mysticism. Nasr states as follows:

"Islam is at once a religion and a civilization and social order based upon the revealed principles of the religion. It is an archetypal reality residing in the Divine Intellect and an unfolding of this reality in history and in the lives of numerous generations of men from different races and ethnic groups and different localities spreading over most of the surface of the earth."

(Nasr 1981 Page 8)

Nasr insists that Islam is both an exoteric and an equally valid esoteric pathway to God realization. Its' ortho-praxis is founded upon its multi-faceted nature of being a religion, civilization and social order. What enables it to be both an esoteric and exoteric pathway to God realization is the transcendent existence of the Divine Intellect and the manifestation of this archetypal reality across history through the mechanism of revelation. The basis of this archetypal reality is the flow of knowledge to man via language/and the text that stands outside the epistemology of man made knowledges. Nasr therefore states as follows:

"Religion may be considered ultimately as the Divine Guide by the help of which man can overcome the ontological barrier separating him from his divine origin, although in essence he has never been separated from it."

(Nasr 1981 Page 8)

Nasr locates the barrier to the human immersion/oneness with the Divine Intellect as being located at the level of the ontological. In essence, the state of separation from the Divine Intellect is then driven by an ontology of being which can not only deny the archetypal reality, but also the path/tariqah to tawhid/Unity/Oneness with God. For Nasr there are therefore epistemologies, ontologies, worldviews of unbelief that ultimately prevent God realization. The path to tawhid/Unity or God realization is then located at the level of language, discourse and text for there is an ontology of belief and God realization. What then is this ontology of belief for Nasr? He states as follows:

"If we put aside the erroneous and truncated concept of man as a creature formed only of body and mind, a concept that is due more than anything else to Cartesian dualism along with a misunderstanding of certain tenets of scholasticism, and return to the traditional conception of man as being comprised of body, soul and spirit.... the relevance of the spiritual states become clear."

(Nasr 1972 Page 68)

Nasr's ontological barrier to God realization is then any ontology that denies the tripartite nature of humans, but more so Nasr insists that it is Cartesian dualism that lies at the foundation of this ontological fallacy. For him the denial of the soul, inevitably led to the denial of God, which was the potent outcome of Cartesian dualism. When then are these elements of man, the corpus, anima and spiritus? Nasr defines the spirit and body as follows:

"The spirit is like the sky, shining and immutable above the horizons of the soul. It is a world which, although not yet God, is inseparable from him so that to reach it is already to be in the front courtyard of Paradise and the proximity of the divine."

(Nasr 1972 Page 68)

The spirit then transcends the limits of the un-regenerated soul/nafs but it is not one with the Divine Intellect. The spirit by being grounded in the physical realm of the body and soul with its imperfections and the potential for God realization has to await oneness with the Divine Intellect upon separation from the physical realm. Nasr continues:

"The body also bears in its objective and natural existence, although not necessarily in its subjective prolongation in the psyche, the "vestiges of the Creator" (vestigio Dei) so that it can be considered as the temple of the Spirit and can play a completely positive role in the very process of spiritual realization."

(Nasr 1972 Page 68)

The body is then the mechanism through which the spirit grounds itself in the material plane, for through the body the spirit develops its relation to material existence. But the body in its subjective realm of existence at the level of the psyche can remove all traces of "vestiges of the Creator", which means that the Way/Path/tariqah to God deals with the realm of the subjective, the psyche that has turned from God. Therefore the Path to God realization can only address man at the level of consciousness, at the level of language, at the level of discourse. For the spirit already transcends the horizons of the soul, therefore it cannot be the motive force of the methodology of realization/the praxis of realization for it is not grounded in the material consciousness of the human.

Furthermore under those conditions the praxis of realization would then be based on continuing revelation being made to each human seeking the Path/the Way/tari'qah, which then directly challenges the tenet of revelation given through a line of Prophets that culminated in Mohammed (uwbp) preserved and transmitted via the text of revelation; the Holy Quran.

What then does Nasr say of the soul/anima? He states:

> "Man in his un-regenerated and "fallen" state, to use the Christian terminology, is the subject addressed by treatises on spiritual discipline. A man in such a state is precisely one who identifies himself solely with his psychic substance or mind, not realizing that this is but a reflection of the intellect on the psychic plane. He identifies himself with the soul that has not yet experienced the liberating contact with the Spirit and he lives imprisoned in a world of sense; impressions deriving from the body, along with the logical inferences drawn from that world, and in an un-illuminated subjective labyrinth that is filled with passionate impulses."

(Nasr 1972 Page 67-68)

Nasr is therefore insisting that the consciousness of man, the anima in its separation from Divine Intellect cannot attain God realization in itself and for itself. The tariqah to Divine Intellect has to be illuminated via revelation for without revelation, man the anima does not have the epistemological means to conceive, to grasp the Divine Intellect, much less to formulate the Path. Therefore for Nasr the epistemologies/ontologies derived from the consciousness of the anima in an un-regenerative state must be made subservient to the epistemology of revelation; knowledges then have to be made subservient to the revealed knowledge at the level of the human individual.

The Path/tariqah is then the praxis of discursive struggle against the discourses of un-regenerated consciousness at the level of the soul/anima. Nasr states as follows:

> "The spiritual path is none other than the process of disentangling the roots of the soul from the psycho-physical world to which they are attached and plunging them in the Divine. It means therefore a radical transformation of the soul, made possible through the grace of revelation and initiation, until the soul becomes worthy of becoming the bride of the spirit and entering into union with it."

> (Nasr 1972 Page 69)

The methodology of "disentangling the roots of the soul from the psycho-physical world" can only then focus at the level of discourse for revelation grasps the psycho-physical world and subsumes it to its vision. This vision is unattainable through the consciousness founded on the psycho-physical realities of the world, via language and its texts. Therefore the struggle between the un-regenerated soul and its epistemologies founded on the realities of the "psycho-physical world" and the epistemology founded on revelation manifests itself at the level of discursive conflict/contradiction. The end sought is discursive dominance/predominance summed up in the structures of discursive hegemony.

Nasr posits that the methodology/praxis to ensure the discursive hegemony of revelation lies in hierarchical spiritual stations which culminate in victory, in God realization, in the fortieth station or tasawwuf or Sufism. Nasr states:

> "To reach God, the soul must become God like. Hence the significance of the spiritual stations and states that the soul must experience and the spiritual virtues which it must acquire and which mark the degrees of the ascent of the soul toward God. In fact each virtue is a station through which the soul must pass and which it must experience in a permanent way."

> (Nasr 1972 Page 69)

The soul marks its ascent towards tawhid through the acquisition of stages/virtues which mark the development of the soul. In fact it's a mutation from being grounded in materiality, carnality to the state of being one with the Divine Intellect. Nasr states:

> "The end of Sufism is of course to reach God, the Truth/al haqq, and not to acquire a particular station. But since man is not just an intelligence that can discern the Truth and know the Absolute, but also a will, the virtues are a necessary concomitant to the total attachment of man to the Truth."

(Nasr 1972 Page 69)

The virtues are then necessary to the disciplining of the will of man with its ability to choose the carnal world over the spiritual oneness of tawhid.

At this juncture the strains within the Sufi worldview become manifest for it is expressed in language via the concepts of hal (plural ahwal) and maqam (plural maqamat). Maqamat or stations are acquired by the Muslim on the tariqah by dint of hard work, which primarily revolves around continuous study of revelation to ensure that consciousness is made subservient to the discourse of revelation. This process of discursive struggle is manifested at the level of will and praxis. Ahw'al or states deal with the flow of temporary, passing phases of divine gifts bestowed upon believer or unbeliever.

In a state of hal the spiritual ecstasy that ensues through the bathing of the soul in the power of the Divine Intellect enables the faqir or darwish to transcend the praxis of the stations/maqamat. The existence of the ahwal at the level of sensory experiences raises the question if it transcends language hence revelation. For the adepts of the tariqah insist that ahwal are transient states of being and can never be the basis of praxis to attain tawhid.

The fact of the matter is that in the realm of the hal there is but one praxis possible, that is the praxis of experience for the darwish cannot transcend hal for it is not hierarchically structured ever pointing to the summit that is tawhid. The state of being that is hal is then incomparable with the stations of maqam and must be made subservient to maqam if the primacy of revelation, language and discourse is to be preserved.

Herein lies the fundamental conflict between Sufi Islamic discourse and exoteric discourse. For Sufi discourse dares to release the jinn from the bottle for whenever Sufi adepts insist that hal can be made into a permanent state of consciousness then the contradiction reaches the point of conjuncture. For in a permanent state of hal, the ortho-praxis becomes irrelevant and the very basis of the ortho-praxis, revelation is subsumed to ecstasy, states of consciousness that refuse expression via language, discourse.

Nasr himself takes great pain to insist on the desirability of maqam over hal and the faqir have over the years interlaced the praxis of maqam with the ortho-praxis of the exoteric discourse in a bid to ensure that they blend into the landscape of praxis constituted by the Islamic exoteric discourse. Nasr states:

> "In contrast to the fleeting nature of hal the permanence of maqam implies that it can be surpassed only when it is fully possessed and all of its conditions are fulfilled...
> The maqamat are in reality so many states of being or degrees of consciousness leading to union, and they stand related to each other in a hierarchical order so that even when transcended they remain a permanent possession of the seeker who has passed through them."

(Nasr 1972 Page 75)

What then is the ortho-praxis of the faqir when faced with the need to expand the horizons of dar ul Islam through missionary activities or to defend dar ul Islam when faced with the assault of hostile unbelievers especially during European colonial expansion.

The faqir of Islamic discourse carry a proud history of persistent missionary activity towards expanding the horizons of dar ul Islam in keeping with the Quranic injunction that states there is no compulsion in the faith. Sufi mystics spread the faith/din through Africa South of the Sahara, where the boundaries of dar ul Islam are still expanding. Likewise it was the same reality in Indonesia and the Sufi mystics still continue to be at the leading edge of Islamic discourse in these geographic areas of the world.

In the period of aggressive European colonialism during the 19th and early 20th centuries it was the Sufi mystics who were at the forefront of the struggle of Islam against European domination. At the forefront in the struggle against European colonialism in Indonesia were the Sufi mystics as Islamic states launched progressive jihads against successive European colonisers. The Muslims of the state of Atjeh were the vanguard of Islam's struggle against

European domination of Indonesia. Islam's struggle against French colonialism in Algeria commenced in 1832 with jihad under the leadership of Sufi mystics. The Indian mutiny against British colonialism in 1859 was made possible by the resurgence of Islamic discourse in India through the works of Shah WaliUllah, a Sufi mystic.

The list is long and illustrious encompassing jihads against European colonialism with Sufi mystics in leadership positions, in Libya, Sudan, Somalia, and areas of Central Africa. The lesson then to be learnt from the history of Sufi involvement in jihad especially against European colonialism is the need to focus on the potency of the discourse of jihad and martyrdom/Shaheed as it cuts across all streams of discourse that would be reviewed in this corpus of work.

After reviewing Nasr's text on the tariqah to Divine Intellect it would be a grievous misnomer, a fallacy to extrapolate that the Sufi way extols a non-violent path. It is obvious that the inward looking path does not in any way deny the duties of the Sufi mystic as a believer/Muslim to ensure that the integrity of the din is maintained at all times. In Islam, discourse constitutes the perceptions of threats to the faith/din and the response/defence mechanism is contained in the discourse of jihad and shaheed.

By way of conclusion, it is then obvious that the Sufi path is structured on its specific discourse which wages an internal battle with the pull towards sensory non-language based experiences of Baraka/God's grace. The Sufi path is in essence an ascetic path that denies the realities of the consciousness of the un-regenerated soul in order to grasp the consciousness of God revealed through revelation. Given the hegemony discourse constantly seeks to create and maintain within Islamic Sufi praxis it is then obvious why Sufi mystics are ardent missionaries of the faith and protectors of the integrity of the faith.

European colonialism, relentlessly discourse driven and always aggressive in its search for discursive hegemony could have evoked but one response in the faqir; that is jihad and shaheed. Even more so in areas of the world in which Islam found itself in a minority position as in India, Atjeh, and the Philippines.

The most intractable and unrelenting Islamic resistance to Czarist, Soviet and Russian aggression and genocide in Chechnya has sprung up from Sufi Islamic discourse. First it was the Naqshbandi Sufi order led by Shaykh Mansur Ushurma that waged jihad upon Czarist forces in the 1780's. In the nineteenth century it was the turn of Shaykh Imam Shamil to lead the jihad against the Czarist military.

The Qadiri Sufi order appeared in the Caucasus in 1861 led by the Daghestani shepherd Kunta Haji Kishiev. The Qadiris allied with the Naqshbandis would rekindle jihad against the Romanov czars in 1865, 1877, 1879 and in the 1890's. The Bolshevik Revolution of 1917 would result in an intensification of the struggle between the Sufi orders and the kufr state.

From 1917 to 1925 the jihad waged was led by Shaykh Uzun Haji with the aim of creating an emirate of the north Caucasus. In response to Muslim rebellion s in 1940 and in 1943 in Chechnya, Stalin forcibly transported more than one million Muslims from the Caucasus to concentration camps in Soviet Central Asia. The Chechen Muslims spent more than a decade in the concentration camps in Kazakhstan, one arm of Stalin's gulag. But the camps failed to sever the Chechen Muslims from Sufi Islamic discourse and Chechen nationalism as defined by Islam.

In fact during their sojourn in the concentration camps of Kazakhstan for over a decade a new Sufi order was spawned created by the Chechen Sufi Uways 'Vis' Haji Zagiev. The Vis Haji rooted in a Sufi Islamic discourse that was tailored to ensure survival of the din, da'wa and the attainment of a Chechen free state is premised upon an Islamic praxis that constitutes a most potent shahid rooted in a discourse of Islamic total war. In 1957 the exiled Caucasian groups were returned to their ancestral homeland. The returning Chechens would find that a deliberate policy of ethnic cleansing and the suppression of Islam had made them outcasts in their own ancestral homeland.

In this reality the Vis Haji order flourished and became the single most potent enemy of the Soviet Union. Vis Haji's praxis is premised upon engagement with the kufr state rather than withdrawal as seen in the praxis of penetrating the Soviet state agencies of Chechnya even those involved in haraam practises as the production of alcohol and tobacco products. Vis Haji blends Chechen Islamic nationhood with a virulent rejection of Russia and the then Soviet Union. By far the most potent development engineered by the discourse of Vis Haji is the concept of Islamic total war, which transcends gender. Vis Haji empowers Muslim women to take part in zikr and women are shaykhs with their circle of murids/initiates.

Vis Haji has therefore created the structure from which emanates the 'black widow' in Chechnya. The 'black widow' is more than a woman of Chechnya who has lost her husband, children and other family in the jihad against

Russia from December 1994 to 2004 and is now a 'suicide bomber'. At its furthest extent a 'black widow' is a female Shaykh or a murid of the Vis Haji order who is a shahid in the jihad against Russia since 1994. This is a development, which indicates the chasm that separates Vis Haji from Al Qaeda and the need for Russia, the U.S.A and Al-Qaeda to suppress by any means necessary the jihad of Vis Haji.

The slaughter of Beslan in its very military futility points to the futile military adventurism of the discourse of Al-Qaeda rather than the total jihad of Vis Haji. The massacre of Beslan was an action that would be one instance in a stream in a bid by the discourse of Al-Qaeda to hopefully internationalise the engagement in the North Caucasus thereby sucking into the maelstrom the Muslim dominated populations of the Central Asian Republics. Vis Haji has nothing to gain by the internationalisation of the conflict in the North Caucasus and given the oil and gas resources of the Caucasus the decimation of the Muslims of the Chechen in exchange for stable access to the energy reserves is a price the North Atlantic is willing to pay. The slaughter of Russian civilians the current instance being Beslan is the most potent threat to a settlement in Chechnya in favour of Vis Haji and it only serves the interest of the kufr and the spawn of the kufr, Al-Qaeda.

Aslan Maskhadov and Shamil Basayev are the tag team of the Muslim insurgents of Chechnya as Sistani and al Sadr the tag team of the Shia of Iraq. Aslan Maskhadov and Shamil Besayev are both instances of the discourses of Vis Haji. Aslan Maskhadov has outwardly sought to re-establish the hegemony of the praxis of Vis Haji which included an assault on the Wahabis of Chechnya. Maskhadov has clearly indicated that muslim solidarity with the Chechen jihad do not encompass and entail threats to the hegemony of Chechen muslim interests as defined by Vis Haji, herein lies the tension between Maskhadov and Al Qaeda. Maskhadov roots the Chechen Muslim insurgency in the Sufi Orders and the blood ties of the clans thereby showing little or no interest in a discourse of the greater kufr of Al Qaeda.

Shamil Basayev as a military commander of the Chechen Muslim insurgency has perfected the methodology of the hostage situation as an offensive weapon against Russia. Both Maskhadov and Basayev understand that there must be a political settlement to the Chechen insurgency and have used since 1995 during the first Chechen war of the 1990's the hostage crisis as the instrument to force a political settlement to the war with Russia. The second Chechen war of the 1990's that broke out in 1999 saw no change to the tactic but the events of September 11th, 2001 changed dramatically the geo-political realities that impact the ongoing war in Chechnya.

Al Qaeda's military adventurism has now bolstered Putin's resolve to subdue Chechnya militarily by any means necessary to the detriment of a political settlement. Basayev's instrument of the hostage crisis is now evidence to internationalise the war against Chechnya's insurgency because of Basayev's reputed links to Al Qaeda. The reality is that groups other than those under the command of Basayev and Maskhadov are using the instrument of the hostage crisis in the name of Chechen independence. Basayev has articulated the discourse of jihad that transcends national boundaries and the solidarity of the Ummah as he clearly attempts to place the Chechen Muslim insurgency within an Islamic context rather than being a narrow insurgency for ethnic interests.

But Basayev has never adopted any internationalist agenda with its locomotive discourse to the detriment of the paramount strategic imperative, which is Chechen Muslim independence from Russia. Basayev is in no way a minion, a vassal of Al Qaeda's agenda of jihad against the greater kufr. It is Maskhadov's role in the tag team to affirm the discourse and the structures that have served Chechen Muslims in their war for independence since engaging with the Romanovs of Russia since the 18th century. Maskhadov as the instrument of Vis Haji has to ensure the hegemony of the Sufi Orders and the strength of the blood bonds of the clan to ensure the constituting of Chechen Muslim warrior in the battle with Russia irrespective of gender.

It is now necessary to trace this discursive structure of jihad and shaheed through the other streams of Islamic discourse in this section, to finally culminate in a presentation of the discourse of jihad and shaheed from the source of all revelation in Islam, the Holy Quran.

EXOTERIC ISLAMIC DISCOURSE: THE SUNNI STREAM.

The first experience of a work of the exoteric Sunni stream of Islamic discourse would come from "Towards Understanding Islam" by Maulana Sayyid Abul Ala Mawdudi (1903-1979). He relentlessly creates a specific stream of exoteric Islamic discourse that is equivocal in its affirmation of the Prophethood of Muhammad (uwbp) and because of this the need to situate Muhammad's (uwbp) discourse, his ortho-praxis as the centrality of din and Shariah. Mawdudi states:

"Although Islam consists of submission and obedience to Allah, the Lord of the Universe, yet as the only authentic and reliable source of knowing Him and His will and law is the teachings of the True Prophet, we may define Islam as that religion which stands for complete faith in the teachings of the Prophet and unflinching obedience to his ways of life. Consequently, one who ignores the medium of the Prophet and claims to follow God directly is not a "Muslim"."

(Mawdudi 1981 Page 64)

Mawdudi makes little attempt to veil his hostility to the Sufi path as he insists that there can be no alternate path to God other than that revealed to the Prophet Muhammad (uwbp). For it is only through revelation to the Prophet that the Path to God was revealed, therefore without "the medium of the Prophet" there can be no salvation. Revelation made only to the Prophet Muhammad (uwbp) results in the fact that Islam the religion has then to be based on the ortho-praxis of the Prophet Muhammad (uwbp). Mawdudi in writing on the concept of Tawheed states the following:

"The most fundamental and most important teaching of Prophet Muhammad (peace be upon him) is faith in the unity of God. This is expressed in the primary kalima of Islam as "There is no deity but Allah"(la ilaha illallah). This beautiful phrase is the bedrock of Islam, its foundation, and its essence. It is the expression of this belief which differentiate a true Muslim from a kafir (unbeliever), mushrik (one who associates others with God in His Divinity), or a dahriya (an atheist)."

(Mawdudi 1981 Page 65)

The concept of Tawheed defines the boundaries of din, the parameters that are policed by Islamic discourse. For tawheed encloses the space of Islam excluding from its realm those characterized as the realms of the kafir, the mushrik and the dahriya. Mawdudi continues:

"It means that in the whole of the Universe, there is absolutely no being worthy to be worshipped other than Allah, that it is only to him that heads should bow in submission and adoration, that He is the only Being possessing all powers, that all are in need of his favor, and that all are obliged to solicit his help. He is concealed from our senses, and our intellect fails to perceive what he is."

(Mawdudi 1981 Page 66)

Mawdudi asserts the power, the centrality of Allah but also the inability of the actions of man to attain unity with Allah through the strivings of intellect and consciousness devoid of revelation. He repeatedly insists that ortho-praxis driven by revelation is the only path to unity with Allah. Mawdudi states:

"In the teachings of Muhammad (God's blessings be upon him) faith in one God is the most important and fundamental principle. It is the bedrock of Islam and the mainspring of its power. All other beliefs, commands, and laws of Islam stand firm in this very foundation. All of them receive strength from this source. Take it away, and there is nothing left in Islam."

(Mawdudi 1981 Page 76)

It is then Prophet Muhammad's (uwbp) teachings on the concept of Tawheed that is the bedrock of Islam. To deny then the Prophethood of Muhammad (uwbp), the revelation that made him to be the final Prophet to mankind and the teachings of Muhammad (uwbp) as a direct consequence of revelation places one in the realm external to Islam, the realm of Jahiliyya. Mawdudi continues:

"This is why it is now incumbent upon each and every human being to have faith in Muhammad (peace be upon him) and follow him alone. To become a true Muslim (a follower of the Prophet's way of life) it is necessary to have complete faith in Muhammad (peace be upon him) and to affirm that:

(a) He is a True Prophet of God.
(b) His teachings are absolutely perfect, free from any defect or error; and
(c) He is the Last Prophet of God. After him no Prophet will appear among any people until the Day of Judgment, nor is any such per-

sonage going to appear in whom it would be essential for a Muslim to believe."

(Mawdudi 1981 Page 84)

Mawdudi in the passage quoted above has now finalized the concept of Tawheed, for Allah through revelation has presented to humankind the final revelation, the final path to salvation, the final Prophet of God through Muhammad (uwbp). The basis of the ortho-praxis of Islam has then been presented by Mawdudi and he states as follows:

"When you declare La ilaha illallah (there is no deity but Allah), you give up all false deities, and you profess that you are a creature of the One God; and when you add to these words Muhammad-ur—Rasulullah (Muhammad is Allah's messenger) you confirm and admit the Prophethood of Muhammad (God's blessings be upon him). With the admission of his Prophethood it becomes obligatory that you should believe in the divine nature and attributes of God in his angels, in his revealed books, and in life after death, and earnestly follow that method of obeying God and worshipping him which Prophet Muhammad (peace be upon him) has asked us to follow. Herein lies the road to success and salvation."

(Mawdudi 1981 Page 92)

Mawdudi states that the five articles of faith quoted above which are obligatory upon acceptance of the validity and truth of the kalima-e-tayyibah "form the foundation for the superstructure of Islam."

On the articles of faith Mawdudi states as follows:

"The earlier discussion has made it clear that the Prophet Muhammad (peace be upon him) has enjoined us to believe in five articles of faith:

(1) Belief in the God who has absolutely no associate with Him in His Divinity.
(2) Belief in God's Angels.
(3) Belief in God's Books, and in the Holy Qur'an as His Last Book.

(4) Belief in God's Prophets, and in Muhammad (God's blessings be upon him) His Last and Final Messenger; and
(5) Belief in Life and Death.
These five articles make up the bedrock of Islam. One who believes in them enters the fold of Islam and becomes a member of the Muslim community."

(Mawdudi 1981 Page 93)

The five articles of faith define the space of Islam thereby differentiating it from the spaces that are outside Islam. Spaces outside Islam therefore deny the concept of Tawheed and the kalima-e-tayyibah, which flows, from Tawheed. There is then mutual repulsion when contact is made between Islam and the spaces designated under the control of Jahiliyya. How then does the ortho-praxis of Islam replicate itself and police the spaces under its control?

Mawdudi posits that at the level of the individual Muslim practice must flow with the profession of faith or shahadat. Mawdudi states:

"Therefore you will be a full fledged Muslim only when your practice is consistent with your profession, otherwise your Islam will remain incomplete. Now let us see what code of conduct Muhammad (peace be upon him) has taught as ordained by God Almighty. The first and foremost things in this respect are the 'Ibadat-the Primary Duties which must be observed by each and every person professing to belong to the Muslim Community."

(Mawdudi 1981 Pages 93-94)

'Ibadat the concept hinges then on the Muslim's total, absolute, submission to the Will of Allah. Thereby all aspects of the ortho-praxis of Islam are acts of 'Ibadat which permeate the Muslim enabling him/her to dwell in the realm of 'Ibadat perpetually.

Mawdudi states:

"This is the true significance of 'Ibadat, viz, total submission to the pleasure of Allah, the moulding into the patterns of Islam one's entire life, leaving out not even the most insignificant part thereof.

To help achieve this aim, a set of formal `Ibadat (worships) has been constituted which serves as a course of training.

The more assiduously we follow the training, the better equipped we are for bringing harmony between our ideals and practices. The `Ibadat are thus the pillars on which the edifice of Islam rests."

(Mawdudi 1981 Page 94)

The pillars of Islam are therefore the formal structures of worship driven by the concept of totalist worship or `Ibadat. The ortho-praxis of Islam that replicates the community of believers, the Ummah, is driven by the pillars of formal worship and the streams of discourse that ground the process in the language of revelation, in the revealed text, the Holy Qur'an. Discourse then drives the ortho-praxis for it is not an ortho-praxis of silence rather it is grounded in language and a text of centrality.

The five formal forms of `Ibadat are:

(1) Salat or prayer five times daily, practiced within the stipulations of the ortho-praxis.

(2) Saum or fasting once per year during the month of Ramadan must be carried out as prescribed by the ortho-praxis.

(3) Zakat is the annual obligation of payment of a portion of a Muslim's material prosperity to specified recipients. Again the calculation, method and mode of payment, and recipients of the Zakat are all determined by the ortho-praxis.

(4) Hajj or Pilgrimage to Mecca is obligatory once in a Muslim's lifetime to those who can afford. The entire method and process of Hajj is governed by the ortho-praxis.

(5) The defence of Islam.

The fifth pillar of Islam Mawdudi defines as "the defence of Islam" and on this issue I would now focus for it is interesting to experience how Mawdudi conceptualises the defence of Islam within the confines of the ortho-praxis of Islam.

Mawdudi states:

"Though the defence of Islam is not a fundamental tenet but its need and importance have been repeatedly emphasized in the Qur'an and the Hadith."

(Mawdudi 1981 Page 100)

Mawdudi posits that the place of the defence of Islam as one of the pillars of the faith is assured by the emphasis placed upon it by the Holy Qur'an and the Hadith. Secondly, he posits that a specific aspect of the defence of Islam, Jihad, is specifically addressed in the Shariah. He indicates that there is then Jihad that is 'Ibadat and Jihad which is a formal act of the Ummah governed by the Shariah.

Jihad then transcends the realm of 'Ibadat the concept of the formal acts of worship and the methodology of war with the realm outside the control of Islam, (dar ul Harb). Jihad and the methodology of war are then 'Ibadat and as such must be subservient to the rules of Allah governing Jihad as revealed to the Prophet Muhammad (uwbp). Jihad against unbelievers must then be based and carried out on the revealed principles of 'Ibadat for without 'Ibadat Jihad cannot be Jihad.

It would simply be then war between realms that have in common their separation from God. Mawdudi states:

> "Jihad is part of this overall defence of Islam. Jihad means struggle to the utmost of one's capacity. A man who exerts himself physically or mentally or spends his wealth in the way of Allah is indeed engaged in Jihad."
>
> (Mawdudi 1981 Pages 100-101)

This is then Jihad that is 'Ibadat, a form of worship towards the permeation of the entire being of the Muslim through submission to Allah (swt). Mawdudi goes on to show the specific meaning Jihad has in "the language of the Shari'ah." He states:

> "But in the language of the Shari'ah this word is used particularly for the war that is waged solely in the name of Allah and against those who perpetrate oppression as enemies of Islam. This supreme sacrifice of lives devolves on all Muslims."
>
> (Mawdudi 1981 Page 101)

For Mawdudi Jihad used in the Shari'ah describes war fought against the enemies of Islam. He therefore locates Jihad the concept and methodology of war against enemies of Islam within the revelation of Allah to the Prophet Muhammad (uwbp) and the Hadith.

Mawdudi can state as follows in light of the above:

> "Jihad is as much a primary duty of the Muslims concerned as are the daily prayers or fasting. One who shirks it is a sinner. His very claim to being a Muslim is doubtful. He is plainly a hypocrite who fails in the test of sincerity and all his 'Ibadat and prayers are a sham, a worthless hollow show of devotion."

> (Mawdudi 1981 Page 101)

While not being a fundamental tenet the defence of Islam is then specifically addressed via the concept of Jihad in the Shari'ah.

What now follows is Mawdudi's position on the Shari'ah and how that illuminates further the structure of the concept of Jihad. He distinguishes between al-Din, the Faith and the Shari'ah of Prophet Muhammad (uwbp). The five articles of faith, which flow from the kalima "La ilaha illallah", is the basis of al-Din for it is the continuous basis of the prophetic line of succession culminating in the Prophet Muhammad (uwbp).

Each prophet brought with him a specific form of the Shari'ah which was abrogated with the coming of the next Shari'ah in the prophetic line but al-Din remains constant, unchanged for it reflects, teaches the nature of God who is unchanging, constant. The revelation to the final Prophet Muhammad (uwbp) therefore means that the Shari'ah Muhammad (uwbp) brought is the final all encompassing Shari'ah for humankind until the Day of Judgment. Mawdudi states:

> "The process ended with the advent of Muhammad, the last prophet (peace be upon him), who brought with him the final code which was to apply to all mankind for all times to come. Din has undergone no change, but now all the previous Shari'ahs stand abrogated in view of the comprehensive Shari'ah that Muhammad (peace be upon him) has brought with him. This is the climax or the finale of the great process of training that was started at the dawn of the human era."

> (Mawdudi 1981 Page 102)

What then are the sources of the Shari'ah of Muhammad (uwbp)? Mawdudi list's these sources as:

(a) The Holy Qur'an.
(b) The Hadith of the Prophet Muhammad (uwbp).
(c) Fiqh or jurisprudence derived from the Qur'an and the Ahadith.
(d) Tasawwuf.

Of primary concern here is Mawdudi's position on Fiqh. Mawdudi insists that the authenticity of all four schools of Fiqh "goes unchallenged" because of the "unimpeachable integrity of their respective founders and the authenticity of the method they adopted." One is then left to deduce that he is of the opinion that the body of Fiqh is complete and finished works immune from continuous and repeated updating as the need arises. If this is his position he is then insisting that the doors of "Ijtihad are closed" which is a major point of departure separating him from the Shi'i and other Muslims who insist that the door of Ijtihad is open.

On the relation of Tasawwuf to Fiqh Mawdudi states;

> "Thus, the true Islamic Tasawwuf is the measure of our spirit of obedience and sincerity, while Fiqh governs our carrying our commands to the last detail. An `Ibadat devoid of spirit, though correct in procedure, is like a man handsome in appearance but lacking in character, and an 'Ibadat full of spirit but defective in execution is like a man noble in character but deformed in appearance."

(Mawdudi 1981 Page 104)

For Mawdudi tasawwuf is grounded in the ortho-praxis of the Shari'ah for it is impossible to separate it from the Shari'ah and yet have it retain its integrity as a God given concept necessary to the attainment of salvation.

For he states:

> "Tasawwuf, in the true sense, is but an intense love of Allah and Muhammad (peace be upon him) and such love requires a strict obedience to their commands as embodied in the Book of God and the Sunnah of his Prophet."

(Mawdudi 1981 Page 105)

Tasawwuf therefore drives the ortho-praxis of Islam for every act carried out in the prescribed manner governed by the Shari'ah must be combined with the right attitude of submission out of love for Allah (SWT) and his Prophet Muhammad (uwbp). Mawdudi's position is then vehemently exoteric as he relentlessly attacks the Sufi mystics in the text under review. But it is an exoterica which combines dualities of consciousness and ortho-praxis. Specific qualities of consciousness must drive and at the same time be promoted by the ortho-praxis. The ortho-praxis is then driven by the discourse of the Shari'ah and Tasawwuf towards the attainment of the goal of submission of the Muslim, total and complete, as defined and delineated in the Shari'ah.

In speaking of the principles of the Shari'ah Mawdudi states:

> "Broadly speaking, the law of Islam imposes four kinds of rights and obligations upon every man, viz;
> (1) The rights of God, which every man is obliged to fulfil, (2) His own rights upon his own self, (3) The rights of other people over him, (4) The rights of those powers and resources which God has placed in his service and has empowered him to use for his benefit."

(Mawdudi 1981 Page 110)

In the Shari'ah the rights of God transcend all other rights and obligations. In fact the other three kinds of rights and obligations upon man cannot exist were it not for the rights of God. For it is the right of God as creator and saviour of humankind through revelation and the prophetic line to demand, to expect paramountcy. Mawdudi locates Jihad as a right of God and states accordingly:

> "And in Jihad he sacrifices money, material and all he has-even his own life."

(Mawdudi 1981 Page 111)

> "In Jihad a man takes away life and gives it away solely in the cause of Allah. In the same way, in rendering God's rights one has to sacrifice many of those things which man has in his control, like animals, wealth, etc."

(Mawdudi 1981 Page 111)

Jihad then is the right of God to demand that even the life of the believer, the Muslim and the lives of the unbelievers be rendered as the ultimate right of God.

Mawdudi states:

> "The greatest sacrifice in the way of God is made in Jihad, for in it a man sacrifices not only his own life and property in his cause but destroys those of others also."
>
> (Mawdudi 1981 Page 112)

But what prompts God to envisage the need to constitute Jihad as a viable solution to a given problem, as a response to circumstances or trends or patterns of behavior in the physical realm of the believer of Islam?

Mawdudi defines the state of existence, of consciousness that demands Jihad as follows:

> "…. one of the Islamic principles is that we should suffer a lesser loss to save ourselves from the greater loss. What comparison can the loss of some lives-even if they are some thousands or more-bear to the calamity that may befall mankind as a result of the victory of evil over good and of aggressive atheism over the religion of God. Decidedly that is a much greater loss and a bigger calamity, for as a result of it not only the religion of God will run down but the world will also become the abode of evil, immoralities and perversion and life will be disrupted from within and without. In order to escape this greater evil God has, therefore commanded us to sacrifice our lives and property for his pleasure."
>
> (Mawdudi 1981 Pages 112-113)

Herein lies the most profound contribution made by Mawdudi to the development of the Islamic discourse of Jihad. He posits that "the abode of evil, immoralities and perversion", is based on the submission of man to finite man. This order is based on rejection of the paramountcy of God and the need for submission to God. Therefore in the abode of evil, there is no co-existence with Islam, for the very essence of the abode of evil must relentlessly strive to negate Islam.

But moreover, of even more importance Mawdudi insists that no Muslim can allow the abode of evil to seize suzerainty over his/her world. Whenever the suzerainty of Islam over space designated as dar-ul-Islam is challenged by the abode of evil, the Muslim must respond, is obligated by God to resist. The form, the methodology of the war of resistance, Jihad, is mandated by the Shari'ah. Mawdudi describes, conceptualises the abode of evil in the dualist constructs of Jahiliyya/Haikmiyya.

Jahiliyya conceptualises the unthinkable for a Muslim i.e. the domination of a state of consciousness in which man now rejects God and worships man and the finite products of the material civilization of man. Haikmiyya conceptualises the state of relations following the hegemony of Jahiliyya and that is the space of Islam, dar-ul-Islam, forced to exist under a state of domination, the hegemony of Jahiliyya over Islam. Jahiliyya/Haikmiyya conceptualise a state of existence totally anathema to Islam and Muslims.

For Mawdudi; there is but one response open to all Muslims faced with the immanent threat of submission to Jahiliyya and that is Jihad as constituted by the Shari'ah. We can only find the details of what actions constitute a threat of Haikmiyya within the Shari'ah and likewise the ortho-praxis of Jihad can only be found in the Shari'ah.

In his essay titled: "The Punishment of the Apostate" by Sayyid Mawdudi he states as follows:

> "To everyone acquainted with Islamic law it is no secret that according to Islam the punishment for a Muslim who turns to kufr (infidelity, blasphemy) is execution."

(Mawdudi 1994 Pg10)

For Mawdudi apostasy in Islam is punishable by execution but by who? Mawdudi states:

> "All these collectively will assure you that from the time of the Prophet, to the present day one injunction only has been continuously and uninterruptedly operative and that no room whatever

remains to suggest that perhaps the punishment of the apostate is
not execution."

(Mawdudi 1994 Pg11)

The execution of apostates has then to be proved as Islamic policy by
Mawdudi by now presenting evidence supporting his position. But before he
does this he states a position, which indicates the worldview of a Muslim fundamentalist. Mawdudi states:

> "They have not considered that if doubts arise even about such
> matters which are supported by such a continuous and unbroken
> series of witnesses, this state of affairs will not be confined to one or
> two problems. Hereafter anything whatever of a past age which has
> come down to us through verbal tradition will not be protected
> from doubt, be it the Qur'an or ritual prayer or fasting. It will come
> to the point that even Muhammad's mission to this world will be
> questioned."

It is then necessary to execute apostates in Islam to ensure the veracity of
Islam. To fail to police Islam for Mawdudi is then to aid and abet forces that
relentlessly assault the citadels of Islam. Why is then Mawdudi adopting such a
totalist stance on the apostate in Islam? The proof he proffers to support his
position as follows: The citing of Sura 9 Verses11, 12 as the Quranic proof supporting the execution of the apostate. The citing of proof from the Hadith,
which supports his position. The citing of proof from the praxes of the rightly
guided caliphs. The citing as proof the jihad against the apostates by the first
caliph, Abu Bakr Siddiq and the citing of the four schools of fiqh. Mawdudi
presents his proof, which according to him is incontrovertible but insists as
follows:

> "Some people, hearing these discourses from the Hadith and the
> Law, keep on asking: Where is the punishment written in the
> Qur'an? Even though we have demonstrated the presence of this
> order also in the Qur'an in the beginning of our discussion, yet, for
> the satisfaction of these people, let us suppose the commandment is
> not found in the Qur'an. Still the number of Hadith, the decisions

of the Rightly Caliphs and the united opinions of the lawyers suffice fully to establish this commandment."

(Mawdudi 1994 Pg 17)

Is there support in the Qur'an for the execution of the apostate in Islam? The text he proffers clearly does not support his position on the apostate in Islam. Whilst Sura 2 Verse 272 states:

"To make them walk in the right way is not incumbent on you, but Allah guides aright whom He pleases;"

And Sura 2 Verse 256:

"There is no compulsion in religion: truly the right way has become clearly distinct from error;"

But in the statement under study Mawdudi reveals the discursive construct of Muslim fundamentalism. For he places the taqlid of praxis over the revelation/wahy of the praxis of Allah: the Qur'an. He continues as follows:

"We ask those who deem this evidence insufficient and request some Quranic reference to prove the existence of this commandment. In your opinion is the full Islamic penal code the same as that which is found in the Qur'an? If your answer is in the affirmative, it is as if you are saying that apart from those actions, which the Qur'an designates as criminal and for which a penalty is prescribed, no other action will be punishable as a crime. Then consider this matter again. Can you run any government in the world successfully even for one day on this principle."

(Mawdudi 1994 Pg 17)

Mawdudi engages with his critics on the basis that for the sake of governance of an Islamic state apostasy must be stamped out, policed via execution even though no clear Quranic support for his position is proffered. For Mawdudi envisions the Qur'an limited by praxis, revelation limited by time and space. He is therefore propagating the notion that for wahy/revelation to be applicable across time/space it must be interpreted by human action. He therefore makes it incumbent upon revelation to ensure its relevance across space/time through human interpreters that arise to create the praxis that revelation is incapable of creating. This elite must then adjudge human action not forbidden by the Qur'an, the human creators of the praxis for revelation. His discourse by extension questions the Tawhid of Allah (swt) hence it is immersed in shirks. He then reveals his position that the execution of apostates in Islam is only applicable within the limits of an Islamic state. Mawdudi states:

> "None of Islam's penal laws can be applied when the Islamic state
> (or, in term's of the Shari'ah, the 'sultan') is not existing."

(Mawdudi 1974 Pg 28)

For Mawdudi it is only when an Islamic state exists that the policy of the execution of apostate is applied. Why? If Islamic law is only applicable within the confines of an Islamic state what then applies to Muslim minorities living in the West especially the North Atlantic? Is then even the very praxis predicated upon human action that he insists renders wahy/revelation relevant across time/space limited in its applicability by its hegemony over geographical spaces. He is then insisting that Islam is condemned to seize, to hold geography over which the Shari'ah is applied. In the absence of geographic hegemony Islam is then rendered flawed, even impotent. For what is Haraam according to Mawdudi in an Islamic state flouts the Shari'ah in the land of Jahiliyyah. Why then is apostasy punishable by death in the Islamic state for him? He states as follows:

> "where religion itself is the ruler, where religious law is state law,
> where religion has taken into its own hands the responsibility of
> maintaining peace and order, does or does not religion have the
> right to punish those who have promised loyalty and obedience to
> and then turn away. We answer this question in the affirmative."

(Mawdudi 1994 Pg 28)

Mawdudi is then insisting that the Muslim living within the confines of an Islamic state swears allegiance to the state religion. To then walk away from one's oath of allegiance is to be launching an attack on the hegemony of the state demanding execution. For the state and Islam are one for the state is the expression of the praxis of human action that affords revelation/wahy the condition of being absolute. That is why in the absence of hegemony over warm bodies geographically delimited, the Islamic laws that apply to such a reality simply remain a potential within the praxis that limits Allah (Allah forbid). What Mawdudi is positing as the Islamic state is in fact an autocracy that polices the Muslims of this state based upon a discourse of law that demands the power to intervene between Muslim and Allah (swt). It is an autocracy predicated upon the rebellion against Allah's praxis for Allah's praxis expressed in a book means that each and every Muslim must be grounded in Allah's praxis through literacy, through individual reading of the book that is revelation. The autocrats must always seek to limit Allah's revelation and access to the book by any means necessary.

Surah 49 Verse 17 states:

> "They think that they lay you under an obligation by becoming Muslims. Say: Lay me not under obligation by your Islam; rather Allah lays you under an obligation by guiding you to the faith if you are truthful."

The basis of the hegemony of the autocrats is then a system of discipline and punishment that micro manages the daily life of the Muslim to the point where the Muslim is estranged from the praxis of Allah for the book is estranged from the Muslim and vice versa.

Mawdudi elucidates the autocracy of the 'learned men' when in the text under review he describes the methodology of the Islamic revolution as follows:

> "In my opinion its solution—and God conforms us to rectitude-is to notify the Muslim population in the area where an Islamic revolution occurs that people who in belief and practice have defected from Islam and wish to remain as defectors should formally disclose their non-Muslim identity and leave our social order within a year from the date of notification. After this period all those who are born of Muslim lineage will be considered to be Muslim, they will be subject to all Islamic laws, they will be compelled to perform the religious duties and obligations, and then whoever steps outside the

fold of Islam will be executed. Following this announcement utmost effort should be made to save as many sons and daughters born of Muslims as possible from the lap of kufr. Then whosoever cannot be saved by any means should be cut off and cast away, sadly but firmly, from his society forever. After this act of purification a new life for Islamic society may begin with only those Muslims who are dedicated to Islam."

(Mawdudi 1994 Pg 35)

Mawdudi is then by his proposal listed above of the same autocratic worldview as the Khemer rouge of Cambodia. The taliban of Afghanistan, the Khemer rouge of Cambodia and Mawdudi of Pakistan all share a common worldview whose origin is the racist, totalist discourse of the north Atlantic. Mawdudi and the Deobandis show the common colonial heritage they share as with the ideologues of the Khemer Rouge as Pol Pot indicating the reality that both he and the Deobandis have masked their discursive antecedents from Europe with a veneer of Islam. His concept of the Islamic state is but the state envisioned by atheist, secular, racist discourse of the north Atlantic masked in a veneer of Islam.

The very discursivities of Islamic discourse were never unearthed by him and utilized as the basis of articulating the alternate discourse of Islam's anti-state. He therefore creates a stream of discourse that serves as a Trojan horse that enables the suppression of Islamic discourse by orientalist, racist, north Atlantic discourse. What is then termed resurgent Islam, militant Islam, Islamic fundamentalism is in fact the most potent expression of self-immolation, within the Ummah since the Crusades. A stream of Islamic discourse that wraps western secular, atheist, racist, sexist discourse with a veneer of Islamic thought illustrates that in Islamic fundamentalism Islam has surrendered to the western colonizers at the level of the idea.

Rather than an Islamic resurgence Islamic fundamentalism is in fact the final battle between Islam and Jahiliyyah for hegemony, with Islamic fundamentalism being the most recent incarnation of Jahiliyyah western style. The Islamists seek to trap the Ummah in a praxis in which the book of revelation is estranged from the Ummah and a totalitarian state in the interest of a visible minority ruthlessly micromanaging the daily lives of the inmates of this state all in the name of God. This brand of fundamentalism is one of a stream of discourse in Islam that continues to surrender to the west at the level of the idea since the earliest instances of contact between Islam and the west.

In addition to autocratic repressive social structures the Islamists have now bequeathed to the Ummah military actions against the west that not only endanger the integrity of the Ummah in the west, it destroys the agenda of da'wa in the west. Military action, in the tradition of the futility and stupidity of the Japanese attack on Pearl Harbor, on the west as the attack on New York ultimately works to the benefit of Jahiliyyah. For it invites Jahiliyyah to assault the Ummah militarily and at the level of the idea whilst the agenda of da'wa and Islamic intellectual resurgence is relentlessly postponed and delayed by the assault of Jahiliyyah and their spawn in Islam. It is impossible to engage with Jahiliyyah and defeat Jahiliyyah when at the level of the idea we utilize the discursive constructs of the enemy.

Islam has failed to address the realities of the impact western colonialism has had upon the Ummah and our subsequent failure to purge ourselves of the ideas of Jahiliyyah. The Ummah is then at its weakest at the point in its post colonial existence when the spawn of western Jahiliyyah, the most powerful and intractable enemy ever faced by Islam, has engaged with the west in a futile act of military adventurism that threatens the viability of the Ummah and the mandate handed down to the Ummah in the Qur'an: the mandate of da'wa. Surah 2 Verse 251:

> "And were it not for Allah's repelling some men with others, the earth would certainly be in a state of disorder."

The text: "The Resurgence of Islam and our Liberation from the Colonial Yoke" by Miriam Jameelah 1980 is an example of the application of Maulana Sayyid Mawdudi's concepts of Islam to a specific issue i.e. liberation of the Ummah from neo-colonial domination. Jameelah's position is that the arrival of the 15th century of the Hijri calendar has found the Ummah faced with the ever-present threat of absorption into Western civilization. Jameelah states:

> "Along with all other non-European peoples of the world, we fell under foreign colonial domination and are now in the post-colonial period being speedily absorbed into the mainstream of modern Western civilization."

(Jameelah 1980 Page 5)

Moreover and perhaps what is most painful to Jameelah is that under the period of post-colonial "independence" the drive to embrace "Western civilization" is being propelled by the colonized to the detriment of Islam. Jameelah states:

> "Indeed we can argue with considerable justification that the post-colonial period we are living in now is in fact only a continuation of the colonial period that government by local westernised elites, which persecute Islam and true Muslims, is nothing but colonialism from within. None of the Muslim states have been able to solve any of the social, economic, political or cultural conflicts inherited by them from colonialism."

> (Jameelah 1980 Pages 6-7)

The inability of the westernised elites to address the legacy of colonialism much less to resolve them for Jameelah is vindication for her resistance to their vision on the basis of it being non-Islamic. Under the rule of the anti-Islamic westernised elites of dar-ul-Islam the pace and velocity of the relentless attacks upon the Muslims has quickened through the perfection of the weapon of cultural imperialism. Jameelah states:

> "Since cultural imperialism has replaced direct political intervention, the consequences are far more devastating in the present than in the past. Western ideals and values, or more accurately, the lack of them, are exported to the Muslim world by means of the imported films, radio and television programmes…"

> (Jameelah 1980 Page 10)

What is the role of this assault via mass popular culture in the assault upon Islam? Jameelah states:

> "The cultural invasion via the mass-media is far more effective in destroying our indigenous life-style than previously conducted through their educational systems alone because this affects the

illiterate masses of peasants and workers whereas formerly during the colonial period, it reached only a tiny privileged elite."

(Jameelah 1980 Page 10)

The result of this relentless attack of Western civilization is manifest according to Jameelah throughout the Ummah as she states:

> "The result is the complete erasing of our historical heritage and the relentless erosion of our identity as Muslims. The breakdown of our society thus continues at an ever-accelerating pace, producing a new generation of rootless, cynical and alienated people. The results of our abject slavery to the colonial yoke in the post-colonial era can be clearly seen everywhere."

(Jameelah 1980 Page 16)

But for Jameelah who is the progenitors, the anti-Muslim fifth column situated within the Ummah who continue to facilitate the assault of western civilization upon dar-ul-Islam? She identifies the fifth columnists as the westernised or educated elite, the product of colonialism but moreover she cites the concepts of "modernization", "development", and "progress" as being the weapons utilized by the westernised elite and their former colonial overlords in their relentless attacks upon the Ummah. Jameelah states:

> "Under the colonial yoke, systematic brain-washing of the educated elite made them in evaluating their former rulers, forget and entirely overlook the genocides, exploitation, tyranny, cultural and spiritual devastation and countless atrocities committed on their people by the imperialists. Indeed they accept the cultural consequences of colonialism and even welcome it eagerly. Instead of the "white man's burden" and Europe's "civilizing mission" to the "benighted East", the colonial yoke is today justified and expended under the slogans of "modernization", "development" and "progress"."

(Jameelah 1980 Page 18)

Jameelah's struggle is then two fold, firstly there is the struggle to liberate the Ummah from the rule of the westernised brain-washed elites and secondly there is the need to create an Islamic epistemology/paradigm/worldview that engages the epistemology/paradigm of Western civilization. From here on in her text she devotes herself to both problematics. On the first problematic she insists that the resurgence of Islam against the rule of the westernised ruling elite began with the Islamic Iranian Revolution in 1978.

With the success of the Islamic Iranian Revolution in overthrowing the westernised elite of Iran thereby halting the advance of western civilization in Iran, the momentum must be stepped up. Jameelah states:

> "Who could have possibly foreseen at that time that an obscure, frail, aged religious scholar living alone in exile-Imam Ayatollah Khomeini-could lead a revolution.... and usher in a completely new order, repudiating nationalism and secularism, promoting Sunni-Shi'a amity, proudly and openly based on Islam."

> (Jameelah 1980 Page 22)

In light of the victory of the Islamic Iranian Revolution what then is the strategy to maintain the momentum of the wave of change?
Jameelah's strategies call for (a) revival and propagation of the memories of the Mujahideen who resisted European colonial expansion with their lives, (b) relentless assault on the western concepts of nationalism and the nation state. (c) Propagation of the movement to re-create and review the Khilafat.

She states as follows:

> "In our struggle to liberate ourselves from the colonial yoke, we must revive the memories of all our great valiant Mujahideen who struggled against European imperialism...The memories of their heroic deeds must be revived and retold in all the school texts for our children and youth to inspire our leadership for the future."

> (Jameelah 1980 Pages 22-23)

Jameelah is now insisting that a cross-fertilization of the Shi'i methodology of resistance with the Sunni desire for liberation. The creation of a specific discourse of the Mujahideen with its texts must be created within the Sunni Ummah as a vital and necessary instrument in its struggle for liberation from the colonial yoke. The struggle against nationalism and the nation state has then to be waged on the basis of Jihad through the Mujahideen, but why does she reject nationalism and the nation state? Jameelah states:

> "Our Muslim brethren in all new nations are being subjected to a new religion-nationalism. They are forced to worship their country and its leaders. National Day, Republic Day and the Day of the Revolution holds more importance than the Islamic Eids. Saluting the national flag and rising to our feet to sing the national anthem has become a substitute for Salat."

> (Jameelah 1980 Page 24)

Jameelah's position is that the symbols and rituals of nationalism are seeking to displace the ortho-praxis of Islam. Nothing within the space of Islam can replace, make subservient to itself the 'Ibadat' of Islam. That condition is then harkening to the return of Jahiliyya/Haikmiyya and can only result in one reaction by Muslims: Jihad. She states:

> "If the Islamic revolution is to achieve success it is imperative that nationalism and the concept of the nation state be repudiated absolutely..."

> (Jameelah 1980 Page 25)

On the Khilafat Jameelah's position is that given the existence of liberated zones of dar-ul-Islam the move now must be made to link these liberated zones under the leadership of the Khilafa. She states:

> "The aim must not be narrow exclusive national sovereignty but Muslim unity and the revival of the Khilafat. Once Khilafat is established, Islam will once again become in the next century of the Hijra a powerful political and spiritual force in world affairs."

> (Jameelah 1980 Page 25)

She now tackles the issue of the need to wage war with western civilization at the level of discourse and the epistemology/paradigm that drives discourse. From the outset she refuses to see in the western conquest of the non-European peoples of the world, affirmation of the inherent superiority of the European and the inherent inferiority of non-white peoples. This is impossible for her to envisage in Islam for to do so would deprecate the potency of the revolution that drives Islam. She states:

> "The superiority of the West in energy, organization and technology was in large measure responsible for its' domination over the rest of the world."

> (Jameelah 1980 Page 26)

We of the periphery according to Jameelah succumbed to a virulent strain of Western materialism, which simply infected our societies at a time when we had no developed immunity to this western disease. She states:

> "The Muslims along with all other non-European peoples everywhere, both primitive and highly civilized, succumbed not so much because of their "decadence" or "stagnation" but rather because western materialism is a virulent, malignant disease capable of destroying even a healthy people."

> (Jameelah 1980 Pages 26-27)

Jameelah states that the battering ram of western materialism and secularism is modern science. Modern science was used since the European Renaissance to repudiate theology thereby opening the way for the hegemony of materialism. Modern science and technology is then driven by godless materialism, which explains the devastation modern science has wrought upon God's creation. She states as follows:

> "Since the dawn of the European Renaissance modern science has been the most conspicuous product of materialism and secularism as well as its most powerful weapon."

"…it later repudiated all religious beliefs as "superstition" only to become a new religion in itself…"

(Jameelah 1980 Page 27)

"The pollution of the earth is merely the end result of the pollution of the soul with godless materialism."

(Jameelah 1980 Page 28)

Finally in her text Jameelah addresses the issue of the creation of an Islamic epistemology to do battle with western civilization. Jameelah states:

"In order to attain complete liberation from the colonial yoke, it is essential for our scholars to formulate a comprehensive and convincing critique of the scientific myths which have prevailed during the last three centuries."

(Jameelah 1980 Page 28)

The deconstruction of western science must be founded on an Islamic epistemology of scientific knowledge and methodology. Secondly, she insists that part of the process of liberation must be the abandonment of the concepts of western civilization, which continue to reinforce our self-immolation. She states:

"We must cease to judge our countries and our peoples by the criterion of "development"."

(Jameelah 1980 Page 28)

But it is necessary to create an alternate Islamic worldview, which defines, expounds via discourse what is the path of non-western Islamic societies. For only with an alternate Islamic discourse of societal evolution is the Muslim enabled to discard the essentially racist, self-immolating epistemology of the white man. Jameelah next insists that science must be freed from materialism. She states:

> "We must liberate science from the philosophy of materialism, resist its dehumanising effects and unify this fragmented concept of knowledge to begin once again to create a new Islamic science on our own initiative."

> (Jameelah 1980 Page 28)

Finally Jameelah points to a basic tenet of the alternative Islamic world-view. She says:

> "Finally, we must repudiate the erroneous ideal of material progress and well being as the aim of human life."

> (Jameelah 1980 Page 28)

The aim of all human life has to be submission to God's will nothing else. But she goes further than this when she states:

> "We should not allow ourselves to be misled by the delusion that poverty, disease, suffering and death can be eliminated nor should we try to do so but instead we must combat social injustice, political tyranny and help the victims as much as possible wherever we find them."

> (Jameelah 1980 Pages 28-29)

The ability to end suffering, disease and death lies outside the capabilities of humankind, that power belongs only to God. To humankind, to Muslims it is appointed the task of struggle, Jihad, against social injustice and tyranny. On the question of the methodology of Jihad, Jameelah therefore ends her text. For Jihad is the means by which the Islamic revolution would be realized. Jameelah states:

> "According to the Shari'ah, all Muslim men have the right to be armed."

> "We must openly call on all Muslim heads of state to submit to the Shari'ah. Once they have refused, they have admitted the fact to all

that they are nothing more than munafiqin (hypocrites) and must be deposed by the Muslim community as the Shah was deposed in Iran."

(Jameelah 1980 Page 30)

Jameelah then lists the methodology of the constituting of the Mujahideen, a methodology to be noted for its use throughout dar-ul-Islam in the constituting of the Mujahideen.

STAGE 1

"A group of Mujahideen must seclude themselves for intensive training in Islam, Inam and Ihsan."

(Jameelah 1980 Page 30)

STAGE 2

"They must study and recite Qur'an and Hadith until they are thoroughly acquainted with its message and determined to follow its guidance."

(Jameelah 1980 Page 31)

STAGE 3

"They must practice the Dhikr of Allah and keep vigil in Tahajjud prayers during the night. Intensity of Dhikr is a prerequisite for battle."

(Jameelah 1980 Page 31)

STAGE 4

"They must be trained in combat. Tactics are part of war."

(Jameelah 1980 Page 31)

STAGE 5

"When the training in these elements is complete, the Mujahid then goes into solitary retreat for prayer and meditation. If Allah wills, his inner eye is opened and he is freed from fear of his enemies and lack of provisions."

(Jameelah 1980 Page 31)

The methodology towards the production of a specific type of believer, a Mujahid, is driven by discourse, specifically the discourse of Jihad/the Mujahideen/the Shahid. It is discourse that establishes the boundary between Islam and Jahiliyya, Islam and Shirk (polytheism) and consequently between the believers and unbelievers. The realms of belief and unbelief of Muslim and Kuffir are defined and differentiated by discourse within spaces in which Islamic discourse is hegemonic.

The selection, the creation of a group of Mujahideen is discursively driven. But moreso the journey from the stage of the recruit to the Mujahid is even more discursively centered, for the final product of the process is the acceptance and the active seeking out of shahid or martyrdom.

Stage 1: the secluded group of Mujahid must be intensively trained in Islam or al-Din, in Ihsan and in Iman. Ihsan is defined in the Hadith as:

> "Ihsan is to adore Allah as though thou didst see him, and if thou dost not see him he nonetheless seeth thee."

Iman/faith is defined as follows:

> "The merit of faith is fidelity to the supernaturally natural receptivity of primordial man; it means remaining as God made us and remaining at His disposition with regard to a message from Heaven which might be contrary to earthly experience, while being incontestable in view of subjective as well as objective criteria."

(Nasr 1972 Page 36)

Ihsan, Iman and Islam therefore flow along a discursive continuum for without the concepts, the realities of Ihsan and Iman there can be no Islam, no submission to God's will.

Stage 2 bolsters this position for it is a given that the mujahid must be versed in the Sunnah of the Prophet Muhammad (uwbp).

Stage 3 revolves around the Dhikr of Allah. Firstly the Dhikr of Allah is linked directly to Stage 5 which is the stage of meditation/fikir and salat.

Secondly the Dhikr of Allah is defined as follows:

> "The quintessential form of prayer, the Dhikr or invocation, in which all otherness and separation from the Divine is removed and man achieves tawhid..... the Dhikr finishes by becoming man's real nature and the reality with which he identifies himself, with the help of Dhikr, as combined with appropriate forms of meditation or fikr, man first gains an integrated soul, pure and whole like gold, and then in the dhikr he offers this soul to God in the supreme form of sacrifice."

> (Nasr 1972 Page 49)

Dhikr, fikr and specifically Tahajjud salat are the discursive means to realize the state of existence, fit and purposeful, towards the ultimate sacrifice that is shahid in the realm of Jihad. Dhikr then drives the shahid for without that attainment of dhikr there can be no ultimate sacrifice as shahid. It is then discourse that sets the parameters that differentiates the realm of dhikr from states of existence that lie out of the realm of dhikr. Moreover it is discourse that establishes the signposts that indicate to the believer journeying towards dhikr, the status of his journey and the terminus of his journey.

The entire phalanx of perceptive structures that guides the journey of the believer towards the attainment of the goal of ultimate sacrifice is discursively determined. For it is language in its discursive expressions that fostered, that gave birth to the process of dhikr, because in the Islamic worldview the power of silence is inhabited only by the darwishes who are repeatedly placed outside the ortho-praxis of Islam hence they are shirk.

The final stage of the process before the actual engagement of battle within Jihad and martyrdom (shahid) is then the process of tapping the baraka of Allah. This act of grace/baraka of Allah whereby the power of God finally and can only prepare the Shahid, the Mujahid for the Jihad at hand. The methodology of Dhikr, Fikr and Tahajjud salat enables the Muslim to tap into, to be acceptable for the flow of the baraka of Allah.

There is no Shahid, no Mujahid without this flow of baraka for the ultimate sacrifice must be acceptable to Allah for the process of initiation undertaken to have meaning. For the Shahid/the Mujahid in the realm of the material becomes the instrument of Allah in the struggle against that abode of evil and for this ultimate sacrifice reaps the reward of Paradise. But through dhikr the ultimate sacrifice can end with unity/Tawhid with the Divine Essence/Allah.

The entire methodology of the Mujahid quoted by Jameelah is in fact esoteric in purpose and the worldview, therefore of unquestioned Sufi origin. Jameelah is then positing Sufi esotericism as the driving discourse of her methodology of liberation through Jihad. A position that breaks with the Sunni exotericism of Mawdudi and points to the salience of the Islamic Shi'i discourse of Jihad and the Mujahid.

The newspaper the Observer on Sunday September 30th, 2001 printed the four-page document found in the luggage of the suspected leader of the Shahids of the attack on New York of 11th September 2001,Mohamed Atta. The document is strikingly similar to that of Jameelah in its presentation of the methodology of the shahid. Atta's document commences with instructions for the night before the actual event. Atta instructs that ritual cleanliness be practiced such as removing excess hair from their bodies. Atta insists on two core actions: (1) that the shahid be ever mindful of the special relationship that exists between God and the martyr. (2) That the martyr commands train his soul to listen and obey. Atta states as follows:

> "so tame your soul, purify it, convince it, make it understand, incite it."

Atta on prayer states as follows:

> "be persistent in asking God to give you victory, control and conquest,"

On being ever mindful of Allah (swt) Atta states:

> "Remember God frequently, and the best way to do it is to read the Holy Qur'an."

Atta calls for the purification of the soul by purging the soul of all unclean things and of the concerns of daily life. Atta is then calling for transcendence in which the shahid wills himself into a state of deep longing for paradise which severs the ties to this level of material existence. The shahid becomes totally transfixed upon transcending death and the entry into the next level of existence that is Paradise that the action that results in death is welcomed even rejoicing at the moment of death. Atta therefore insists that tranquillity should wash over the shahid then night before the event for as the time draws nigh for the event the Shahids proximity to eternal bliss narrows. Atta then makes a statement that indicates the discourse of the shahid in Islam as follows:

> "Keep in mind that, if you fall into hardship, how will you act and how will you remain steadfast and remember that you will return to God and remember that anything that happens to you could never be avoided, and what did not happen to you could never have happened to you."

The fact they are shahid on the night before their action of martyrdom is what was ordained for them, it is their fate as set by God and it cannot be avoided. The fatalism of Atta's Islam precludes one from action that seeks to relentlessly change human action for what one visualizes as one's reality and the action derived thereof is in fact the fatalistic response of man to the will of God. Atta's role in life is to relentlessly seek out opportunities, which enables liberation from the predestined fatalism of human action through the methodology of the shahid, which ends a fatalistic existence on the material plane for the bliss of Paradise. For Atta engagement with the unbeliever/kuffir to the point of martyrdom is the acceptable price to be paid for release from the circularity of fatalistic futility. This worldview has then to posit unending unrelenting, military engagement with the kuffir. For it is the martyrdom of military engagement with western Jahiliyyah that liberates the fundamentalist from the material plane of existence.

Atta in this vein can then state:

> "All of their equipment and gates and technology will not prevent, nor harm, except by God's will. The believers do not fear such things."

> "for fear is a great form of worship, and the only one worthy of it is God."

It is then the will of God if you succeed in your bid for martyrdom or not only God then is worthy of being worshipped with fear. Pure fear of God then must motivate the male Muslim towards the method of the shahid. Atta states:

> "Do not seem confused or show signs of nervous tension. Be happy, optimistic, calm because you are heading for a deed that God loves and will accept. It will be the day, God willing, you spend with the woman of paradise."

The shahid must then rejoice at the prospect of martyrdom for it is an act that pleases God and is rewarded by God. The action of being shahid is then is a viable methodology of liberation of the Muslim. For as Atta states:

> "and God is with his faithful servants. He will protect them and make their tasks easier, and give them success and control, and victory, and everything."

Atta ends his text by stating:

> "and wholeheartedly welcome death for the sake of God. Always be remembering God. Either end your life while praying, seconds before the target, or make your last words:' There is no God but God, Muhammed is His messenger."

The death of the shahid is then for the benefit of God according to Atta for the shahid is the instrument of God on earth in the never-ending struggle between Islam and Jahiliyyah.
Surah 2 Verse 212:

> "The life of this world is made to seem fair to those who disbelieve, and they mock those who believe".

Surah 2 Verse 214:

> "Or do you think that you would enter the garden while yet the state of those who have passed away before you has not come upon you; distress and affliction befell them and they were shaken violently,"

Surah 2 Verse 286:

> "Allah does not impose upon any soul a duty but to the extent of its ability;"

Surah 3 Verse 145:

> "And a soul will not die but with the permission of Allah; the term is fixed;"

Surah 11 Verse 93:

> "And, O my people! act according to your ability,"

Surah 13 Verse 11:

> "surely Allah does not change the condition of a people until they change their own condition;"

Instances drawn from the Qur'an which indicate that Atta's discourse is premised upon discursive constructs that are in fact extra Quranic. For the textual instances cited insist upon the salience of the action of the human in the path to liberation. The fatalism of Atta's Islam is in no way affirmed or articulated by the said textual instances.

Just as there are instances in which Muslims are excluded/precluded from keeping the fast during the holy month of Ramadan, or making the hajj once in their lifetime to Mecca there are instances where Muslims are excluded/precluded from the pathway of the shahid. Muslims excluded/precluded from martyrdom unlike the position of the fundamentalists does not include women who are Muslims. For all Muslims have the right to claim martyrdom in defence of Islam for Islam teaches total war in defence of Islam. Muslims are precluded from the method of the shahid whenever the act of martyrdom is used in a manner that destroys the potential effectiveness of da'wa. Martyrdom is then a strategy of war between Islam and western Jahiliyyah, called for when the defence of Islam and the Ummah is paramount. The condition of being mujahid and shahid is incumbent upon all Muslims in defence of Islam.

The attack on New York was then totally wrong and indefensible for it effectively destroyed the potentialities of da'wa in the United States and as a strategy of engagement with western Jahiliyyah it was a total failure militarily. A failure for which the Ummah would pay and pay dearly. The hypocrisy of the fundamentalist is apparent for the Palestinian Intifada has raged sacrificing the Muslim youth of Palestine whilst the soft civilian targets of New York were attacked. Whist the Muslim youth of Palestine face the instruments of the racist Zionist order with rocks and sling shots in their hands their Muslim parents stay at home awaiting their corpses to return from the battle lines to wail and cry in public spectacles of funerals shouting that God is great.

There is then an absence of the total war in the defence of Islam in Palestine for the adult Muslims of Palestine are willing to sacrifice their children to evade the condition of being shahid, of being mujahid. Then have then premised their faith in Allah (swt) on a belief in the salience of syncretic, sterile, hybrid Islam for it is liberation by sound bite and the belief that the kuffir can be trusted to deliver Muslims from the grips of the Shaitan. There is only then the boundless living example of the futility of brands that call itself Islam but are in fact the spawn of western Jahiliyyah. For in the midst of their assaults on the west they are the most potent Trojan horses arrayed against the praxis of Allah (swt).

Sayyid Qutb's "Hadha'd-din" or "This Religion of Islam". Qutb's work is of relevance for his presentation of yet another worldview in Sunni exoteric Islamic Discourse. His worldview is premised on the position that mankind through their own exertions which are limited by the capacities and capabilities of the human and the nature of the material conditions under which they exist, would attain salvation. Qutb states:

> "The faith of Islam is a divinely ordained path for human life. Its realization in the life of mankind depends on the exertions of men themselves, within the limits of their human capacities and the material realities of human existence in a given environment."

> (Qutb 1982 Page 2)

For Qutb it is then only through struggle both internally and externally of the human being can there be realization of God's destiny for humankind through Islam. God then responds to this struggle for renewal thereby completing the path of Islam. Qutb states:

> "Truly God does not change the state of a people until they change that which is within themselves."

> "Were God not to repel some people by means of others truly the earth would be corrupted."

> (Qutb 1982 Page 4)

The quotations above are the bedrocks, the lynchpins of Qutb's position. He bases the centrality of struggle both internal and external in the life of the Muslim upon these verses of the Quran. Upon these verses Qutb insists:

> "The truth of the faith is not fully established until a struggle is undertaken on its behalf among people. A struggle against their unwillingness and their reluctance, a struggle to remove them from this state to that of Islam and truth."

> "A struggle by word of mouth, by propagation, by exposition, by refuting the false and baseless with a statement of the truth proclaimed by Islam. A struggle to physically remove obstacles from the path of right guidance when it is infested by brute force and open violence."

> (Qutb 1982 Pages 8-9)

The Muslim has then to internally struggle to subjugate herself/himself to the praxis of Islam likewise externally the environment conducive to the practice of Islam has to be created with struggle. The centrality of struggle in Qutb's worldview is further indicated by his position that struggle, trials, Jihad is utilized by God to continually purge the Ummah of persons who resist the centrality of struggle. Qutb states:

> "Moreover, this struggle and its accompanying trials is the practical means for purifying the ranks of the community-after the initial purification of the individual soul-of ridding it of the idle and the

hypocrites, of those of weak heart and weak character, of tricksters and deceivers."

(Qutb 1982 Page 10)

By way of extrapolation Qutb is then of the position that the purging of the Ummah by God is made necessary by the intransigence and failure of members of the Ummah to create change in themselves and their environment through struggle. Trials and sacrifice levied on the Ummah is then a dynamic path for repeated and continuous change to be continuously visited upon the Ummah. In this dynamic of repeated change through trials God utilizes both internal and external means to replicate the dynamic.

In his text under review Qutb uses the example of the Battle of the Uhud as an example of change wrought through defeat in battle with the Kufir. Again by extension all Jihad between Muslims and Kufir have then internal and external spheres of impact upon the Muslim and the Ummah. A position clearly indicated in the post-July 27th 1990 history of the Ummah in Trinidad. Qutb's position, by extension, holds then that Islam can only realize its destiny within space, territory that is under the control of Islam/dar ul Islam. Qutb states:

> "Islam is a realistic system, and it therefore supposes that the people who live according to its path will be living in an Islamically governed society. In such a society good, virtue and purity will be well known and protected by the leaders of the community. Evil, vice and impurity will be rejected and banished by the dominant forces in society."

(Qutb 1982 Page 32)

What then is the position of the Ummah who find themselves in a minority position within a nation state made up of unbelievers/kuffir therefore ruled by kuffir and based on kuffir law. Qutb states:

> "Those who imagine that the morality of Islam makes of it a heavy burden for humanity so as to prevent its realization in their lives, derive this belief from the tribulations undergone by the individual Muslim living in a society which is not governed by Islam. In such circumstances, the morality of Islam is in reality a heavy burden; it

almost crushes those individuals who live with their pure Islam in the polluted society of ignorance."

(Qutb 1982 Page 32)

The inability of the Ummah to realize through struggle the liberation that Islam supplies is then the most potent evidence of the need for the hegemony of Islam, dar ul Islam. In fact Qutb cannot envisage a section of the Ummah stranded, beached in the society of ignorance/Jahiliyya being able, no matter how earnest their struggle, to realize the liberation of Islam.

What then is the Ummah in Trinidad and Tobago to do in Qutb's world-view? To create syncretic measures such as nationalist credos, racist credos are all shirk for they deny the principles of Islam. The alternatives are then repatriation/mass migration to dar ul Islam or to struggle relentlessly for the creation of dar ul Islam through da'wa/missionary activity or Jihad when the kuffir indicate by their actions that war is now inevitable.

Qutb states on this issue:

"Therefore whoever wishes to be a Muslim should know that he cannot devote himself to his practice of Islam except in a Muslim environment dominated by Islam. He is mistaken if he imagines that he can realize his Islam as an individual, lost in the midst of a society ignorant of divine guidance."

(Qutb 1982 Page 34)

The Ummah caught in a minority position in a society/territory under the dominance of the Kuffir is then a most intractable problematic for Qutb and dar ul Islam. A problematic that has created the most potent hot spots along the frontiers of contact between dar ul Islam and dar ul Harb, throughout the history of Islam to the present day. He differentiates between the Realm of War and the Realm of Islam on the basis of the rule of the Shari'ah and Kuffir law.

Dar ul Islam has then nothing to do with the dominance of the Ummah within the demography of the realm/society. The hegemony of the Shari'ah regardless of the profile of the beliefs of the population includes the territory, realm, and society in dar ul Islam. India under the rule of the Mughal Empire was then dar ul Islam, whereas India under the rule of British colonialism became dar ul Harb.

Trinidad and Tobago has always been and remains dar ul Harb up to the time of writing. Qutb states:

> "The lands ruled by the system of Islam and governed according to the Law of Islam are regarded as the "Realm of Islam" (Dar al Islam) irrespective of whether their inhabitants have all embraced the faith or some of them follow other religions. The lands not ruled by the system of Islam and not governed according to the Law of Islam constitute the "Realm of War" (Dar al Harb), whatever their inhabitants may be."

(Qutb 1982 Page 89)

Moreover, Qutb's position posits that within areas, realms, spaces traditionally designated as dar al Islam, are in fact dar al Harb given the non-governance of the Shari'ah. The best examples of this state of existence are Egypt, Tunisia and Algeria. What then is the role of Jihad in ensuring the continued existence of spaces under the hegemony of the Shari'ah? Qutb states:

> "God imposed the duty of Jihad on the Muslims not so that they might force people to embrace Islam, but rather so that they might erect on earth its righteous, just and sublime system. People might choose the belief they wished in the protective shadow of this system, which embraced both Muslim and non-Muslim in perfect justice."

(Qutb 1982 Page 89)

Jihad is not then a mechanism for conquest of territory/space or the forceful conversion to Islam for Qutb insists that the Holy Qur'an forbids forceful conversion even compulsion in religion. (See al-Baqara 256). Jihad is then envisaged as the primary means for establishing, creating the hegemony of the Shari'ah when war with the Kuffir is inevitable, unavoidable. All else such as territorial expansion is then secondary to the creation of the hegemony of the Shari'ah.

What then is the reality of an Islamic minority besieged by a hostile Kuffir state with no hope of the Ummah being successful to the point of creation dar ul Islam when engaged in Jihad with the hostile Kuffir state? Qutb provides no answers for this dilemma, in fact the Ummah placed in such a reality has to strenuously consult the Sunnah of the Prophet Muhammad (uwbp) to find solutions to such a reality within the ortho-praxis of Islam.

By way of conclusion Qutb's text reviewed is but an indication of Sunni exotericism, which insists on an active ortho-praxis as being the foundation of the path of salvation that is Islam. In his exposition of the concept of struggle both internal and external, he raises the thorny issue of the path of Islam and its potency to enable salvation when under the hegemony of Jahiliyya in the dar al Harb. He emphatically insists that for the Ummah to realize salvation under the hegemony of Jahiliyya is problematic at best.

What then is the Muslim minority to do in such a situation especially when faced with a hostile Kuffir state? Qutb is deafeningly silent on this issue as are all the other Sunni exotericists as Mawdudi and Jameelah.

SHI'I ISLAMIC DISCOURSE.

Shi'i Islamic discourse and its relevance to Muslim minorities situated in dar ul Harb lies in its status within Islam as a minority grouping traditionally faced with hostility from the majority Sunni grouping. Shi'i Islamic discourse has not only constantly replicated its differences with Sunni Islamic discourse, but has had to constantly respond to Sunni hostility by ensuring the survival of Shi'i Islam. How it has responded to its minority status in a hostile environment is seen in specific discursive measures of resistance and replication developed as survival strategies. Shi'i Islam is therefore of relevance to this work for it is today the most potent response made by Islam in a minority position.

Hamid Enayat in "Modern Islamic Political Thought" in writing on Shi'i Islam states as follows:

> "…. perhaps the most outstanding feature of Shi'ism is an attitude of mind which refuses to admit that majority opinion is necessarily true or right, and-which is its converse-a rationalized defence of the moral excellence of an embattled minority."

> (Enayat 1982 Page 19)

Shi'i Islamic discourse supports this position by reference to the Holy Quran (see Sura 6:116, Sura 7:187, Sura49: 4, Sura5: 103).

Sura 2:249 Says:

> "How oft, by God's will hath a small force vanquished a big one?
> God is with those who steadfastly persevere".

Enayat's second feature of Shi'i Islam is the blending of Islamic esotericism with Shi'i theosophy to produce Shi'i Islam, which is driven by dualist notions of binary oppositions.

Enayat states as follows:

> "According to one of the most fundamental principles of Shi'i theosophy, the truth of Islam, like the archetypal reality of all things in the sensible world, can be found only in the mundus imaginalis. So the worldly manifestations of Islam merely reflect part of its truth. Its full truth is only known to God, the Prophet and the members of his house. This doctrine has given rise to a set of dual notions, or binary oppositions, across the whole spectrum of Islamic sciences."

> (Enayat 1982 Page 22)

Shi'i theosophy thereby creates the basis of the hierarchy through which knowledge is transmitted through the ages of man. The All Knowing God, the Prophet (uwbp) and members of his house hold the totality of the Truth (Al-Haqq). With the death of the final male members of the House of the Prophet (uwbp) the Truth/Al-Haqq was then passed to the Executors of the Trust of the Prophet (uwbp) namely the Imam and in the absence of the Imam to the mujtahids. In the absence of the progeny of the male line of the House of the Prophet (uwbp) the Imam in Shi'i Islam has attained discursive prominence unlike Sunni Islam.

This is so because of three discursive constructs, which drive the theosophy. These are:

(a) Ima~mah, Ima~mate revolves around the question of leadership in the Ummah in the absence of the Prophet (uwbp). The Shi'i insist that given God's benevolence and justice to his creation in the absence of the Prophet (uwbp) leadership would not be left undecided by God.

Therefore God would create means and ways to ensure leadership in keeping with his vision for the Ummah.

(b) Wilayah.

In keeping with the concept of the Ima~mah God cannot leave Wilayah or custodianship of the Ummah undecided. The process of selection and leadership is paramount to the mission of Islam hence it cannot be left up to the consensus (ijma) of the Ummah.

(c) Ismah

This is the ultimate test of the qualities of the individual chosen for leadership for Ismah is the degree of the knowledge of God the individual possesses thereby ensuring his impeccability and infallibility.

These three concepts therefore ensure the hierarchy of leadership and the powered structures charged with the production of Shi'i Islamic discourse. The concept of the Imam as the possessor of Ismah in the absence of the Prophet and his progeny is then the locomotive of Shi'i Islamic discourse. For Shi'i discourse replicates its resilience through history by the continuous flow of Ismah, which validates discourse in its every encounter in the discursive realities of human existence.

In the absence of the Imam until the return of the Mahdi, the mujtahid is charged with the task of replicating Shi'i discourse without the intervention of, the flow of 'Ismah. In Shi'i Twelver Islamic discourse the Twelve Imams are then each one the ma'sum or the infallible one, with the Prophet Muhammad (uwbp) and his daughter Fatima being the "Fourteen Impeccables/Chahardah Ma'sum". The centrality of the Imam in Shi'i Islamic discourse is taken to its maximum development with the concept of the return of the hidden Imam, the Mahdi, and the Rehabilitation of the Universe. Twelver Shi'i discourse therefore posits that the victory of Islam over the "forces of injustice" or Jahiliyya is assured with the return of the hidden Imam, the Mahdi.

There is therefore no looking back to a lost Golden Age of Islam as in Sunni discourse. Shi'i discourse relentlessly points to the Golden Age to come and the means to ensure that it becomes an achievable reality.

Enayat states:

> "This link between the Return and the ultimate, global sovereignty of the righteous and the oppressed makes Shi'i historicism a potential tool of radical activism."

(Enayat 1982 Page 25)

The third feature of Shi'i Islam is the centrality of position given to Ijtihad in the fiqh/jurisprudence of Shi'i Islamic ortho-praxis. The centrality of position given to Ijtihad or independent judgment flows logically out of the concept of Ismah and the Ima~mate for in the absence of the Imam, the mujahids is called upon to incessantly update the jurisprudence that secures the perimeters of the ortho-praxis with Jahiliyya.

Ijtihad grants to the mujtahid the flexibility, the ability, the right and duty to expand the boundaries of the ortho-praxis into spaces hitherto unknown/unrealised. Enayat states:

> "Shi'i vitality can be explained primarily by some of its potentiali-
> ties for adaptation to social and political change. The most essential
> of these are the principle of ijtihad or independent judgment, as a
> device supplementing the sources of the jurisprudence and a poten-
> tially revolutionary posture in the face of temporal power."

> (Enayat 1982 Page 160)

Enayat therefore lists the obligation to practice ijtihad by the mujtahids of Shi'i Islam as one of the potentialities for adaptation to social and political change by Shi'i Islamic discourse. At the level of the ortho-praxis of Islam the Shi'i position afforded ijtihad in the mechanism of renewal and replication of fiqh that drives the ortho-praxis sharply demarcates Shi'i Islamic ortho-praxis from Sunni ortho-praxis. Sunni fiqh has insisted that the door of ijtihad is closed raising the issue of the limitations of a static fiqh to come to grips with modernism and secularism.

The question of even more importance to the Ummah placed in a minority position in a state perceptibly hostile to Islam is: "How does the Ummah defend the parameters of the ortho-praxis from the incursions of Jahiliyya with a fiqh that is static, locked in a time warp?"

This is a debate that is driven by the insistence of the traditionalists that the fiqh of Sunni ortho-praxis is in effect complete and perfect. Sunni traditional-ists are then discernible from the Shi'i on their position on fiqh and ijtihad thereby indicating the Orientalist fallacy of lumping the Sunni and Shi'i tradi-tionalists as Muslim fundamentalists', which is just another version of "homo Islamicus".

The fourth element of Shi'i Islam, which not only distinguishes it from Sunni Islam but also affords it relevance to the Ummah in dar ul Harb, is the concept, the discourse of Taqiyyah. Enayat states:

> "Etymologically, taqiyyah comes from the root waqa, yaqi in Arabic, which means to shield or guard oneself, the same root from which the important word taqwa (piety or fear of God) is derived."

> "The Shi'i case for the necessity of taqiyyah is based on a common-place "counsel of caution" on the part of a persecuted minority."

> "…Hence the inclusion, in almost every classical work of jurisprudence (fiqh), of a chapter which either justifies or outlines the rules of the taqiyyah."

> (Enayat 1982 Page 175)

Taqiyyah is then for Enayat part of a strategy for survival of an embattled minority within Islam. Taqiyyah is located within the fiqh of the ortho-praxis which means that (a) it must be supported by exegesis of the texts of the Holy Quran, (b) it must be defined, limited by rules, therefore the bounds and practice of taqiyyah must be in itself an ortho-praxis. In regards to (a) three instances of the text of the Holy Quran are cited: Sura 3:28, Sura 16:106 and Sura 40:28.
(c) The fiqh of taqiyyah enumerates four categories of taqiyyah. These are (1) the enforced/ikrahiyyah,
(2) precautionary or apprehensive/khawfiyyah,
(3) arcane/kitmaniyya, and (4) symbiotic/mudarati. The enforced form of taqiyyah deals with obeying the rules of an oppressor towards saving the lives of the believers.

The precautionary/apprehensive form enables the Shi'i to obey the fatwas of the Sunni. The arcane form enables the Shi'i Ummah to conceal their faith, their ideology, in fact all information on the Shi'i Ummah to the extent of suspending da'wa/missionary activities. The symbiotic form enables the Shi'i to live in peace with the Sunni majority by outwardly practicing Sunni ortho-praxis.

Does the ortho-praxis of taqiyyah enable a Muslim to denounce Islam and embrace the realm of Jahiliyya for the sake of the survival of the Ummah? On this issue upper limits to the ortho-praxis of taqiyyah are placed by the Mujtahids of the Usuli-ifiqh. For taqiyyah taken to its outermost extent can involve revocation of Islam for Jahiliyya which is inconceivable in Islam. The outermost limit is then established by the Mujtahids with the Quranic concept of enjoining the good, and forbidding the evil/al-amr bil-maruf wan-nahyan al-munkar. Taqiyyah transcends the limits of Islam when the believer's actions enter the realm of enjoining evil and forbidding good.

The fifth element that distinguishes Shi'i Islam is the discourse of martyrdom. The martyrdom of Imam Husayn on the plains of Karbala' in the month of Muharram, assumes relevance to various spheres of discursive action. The martyrdom of Husayn presents an expanse of meanings to be interspersed with discourse for specific ends. This was clearly manifested as the prime weapon used against the Shah during the Islamic Iranian Revolution.

When fused with the concept of Jihad, and Shahid, the martyrdom of Husayn frames Jihad and martyrdom within the socio-historical specificity of Husayn.

Discourse then blends the stipulations of the ortho-praxis with the imagery, the actions, and the traditions of the ultimate martyr Husayn. This discourse of Husayn the Shahid is another mechanism that neutralizes taqiyyah in the Shi'i ortho-praxis of Islam. For whenever the Ummah in its practice of Taqiyyah tests the limits of Islamic praxis one can only resort to Jihad to restore the balance or re-frame the basis of the struggle.

Enayat frames the martyrdom of Hussayn accordingly:

> "From a political standpoint, the drama is significant for two reasons; first, Husayn was the only Shi'i Imam in the Twelver school who died in consequence of combining his claim to caliphate with an armed uprising."

> "...Second, the element of martyrdom in the drama obviously exercises a powerful attraction for all Shi'i movements challenging the established order. Husayn is thus the only Imam whose tragedy can serve as a positive ingredient of the mythology of any persecuted but militant Shi'i group of the Twelver school."

(Enayat 1982 Page 181)

By way of summary/conclusion what does Shi'i ortho-praxis offer the Muslim in a minority position within dar ul Harb? In the first instance Shi'i Islam affords an ortho-praxis to specifically deal with unbelievers, kuffir who are perceived as hostile to Islam. Taqiyyah enables the believer to ensure by any means necessary the survival of the Ummah.

The expression and utilization of taqiyyah can very well involve the utilization of kuffir law and jurisprudence to the extent of claiming the rights and obligations of citizens in the specific political entity, including political participation. The use of kuffir law to validate the right of the citizens of the Republic to situate themselves in the ortho-praxis of Islam is but another instance of taqiyyah afforded the Muslim.

The amnesty issue and the Jamaat al Muslimeen is the most potent example of taqiyyah used and utilized by a Muslim minority in a military engagement with an unbelieving nation state afforded in the history of Muslim minorities in the Western hemisphere. For the Jamaat al Muslimeen utilized kuffir law and its jurisprudence to ensure the survival of the believers when faced with at minimum martyrdom at the hands of the kuffir state. The strategy of taqiyyah thereby ensured the survival of the Ummah and the ensuing re-formulation of the system of relations between the Ummah and kuffir in Trinidad and Tobago.

But what of martyrdom as a decisively military action in Jihad? Are there links to the methodology of registering rejection of the present form in which the Muharram at St. James is manifested and the acceptance of the significance of the martyrdom of Imam Husayn to the ortho-praxis of Islam in Trinidad and Tobago?

Protestors at the Muharram have since the mid 1980's insisted that the Muharram is a solemn occasion marking the martyrdom of Imam Husayn. What then is the ortho-praxis of Islam that drives this annual protest since the mid 1980's? Is it a resurgent Shi'i ortho-praxis that has drawn strength from the Islamic Iranian Revolution of 1979 thereby embodying the praxis of the discourse of the martyrdom of Imam Husayn, which must then "take back" the Hosay from syncretic incursions?

Maybe it is a post-Islamic Iranian Revolution 1979 Sunni ortho-praxis, which is striving to claim the legitimacy of the Muharram but not Hosay as, is presently constituted. Or perhaps it is the actions of a minority within an Ummah in a minority position that is consciously seeking to draw from the ortho-praxis of Islam towards the creation of an Islamic ortho-praxis in

Trinidad and Tobago that is relevant to the needs, expansion and survival of the Ummah. These are potent questions to be answered in the chapter that deals with the Islamic ortho-praxis in Trinidad and Tobago.

MUSLIM MINORITIES

The question of the development of Islamic fiqh/jurisprudence that addresses the specific problems of the Ummah in a minority position in a kuffir state is a most potent problematic that continues to engage especially the Ummah minorities in the West.

Central to this debate over the creation of fiqh that addresses the realities of a Muslim's daily life within the hegemony of the white man's Orientalism is the utilization of ijtihad within the bounds of taqlid (tradition). In addition Western Muslim minorities are faced with Streams of discourse, which clearly refuse to understand the specificities of the Ummah's position as minorities within the spaces of the West. These discursive streams blatantly deny the possibility of the ortho-praxis of Islam taking root and being coherently adhered to in the West.This position was deliberately presented in preceding sections, which dealt with Mawdudi, Jameelah and Qutb.

Writers of the rejectionist discursive stream therefore posit that given the hostility of the West to Islam and the difficulty in replicating the ortho-praxis of Islam, thereby the only contact should be via military engagement, persistent Jihad. This position evades the issue of da'wa/missionary activity in the ortho-praxis of Islam. For to disengage from the West and maintain contact via relentless military engagements is self-defeating.

For (a) it offers the minority Ummah in those states as cannon fodder for the anti-Islamic Orientalist elites who are relentlessly seeking to eliminate the viral infection from the Western body politic.

(b) It makes da'wa well nigh impossible for the Ummah simply cannot wage Jihad and carry out the activities of da'wa simultaneously and continuously.

The rejectionist/Jihad stream of discourse coming out of dar al Islam clearly fails to understand the unique dynamic that challenges the existence of Muslim minorities in the West.

What then are the solutions offered to the Muslim minorities by the Holy Quran and the Sunnah of the Prophet Muhammad (uwbp)?

Secondly, how are these Muslim minorities to set about the task of creating a body of fiqh that addresses the daily realities of life in the West?

M. Ali Kettani in his text "Muslim minorities in the world today" 1986 addresses the issues outlined above. Kettani defines a Muslim minority as follows:

> "one may say that a "Muslim minority" is "a part of a population which differs from the rest of the population because its members affirm Muhammad, the son of Abdullah to be the last messenger of Allah and hold his teachings to be true, and which is often subjected to differential treatment by those who do not share the above mentioned belief."
>
> (Kettani 1986 Page 2)

The affirmation of the ortho-praxis of Islam is therefore the basis of the constituting of a distinct Muslim minority entity. The minority is Muslim only by reason of the ortho-praxis of Islam rather than race and ethnicity. Kettani states:

> "Islam discourages a Muslim to acquiesce wilfully to a state of minority if he cannot exercise his right to worship the One True God."
>
> (Kettani 1986 Page 3)

What then are the strategic alternatives offered by the Holy Quran and the Sunnah of the Prophet Muhammad (uwbp)? The examples are all drawn from the actual practices of the Prophet (uwbp) and these are as Kettani states:

> "Therefore, when the right of a Muslim to practice his faith is denied by any power, he must either fight back in self defence, and become a mujahid; or if he cannot fight or fails in this fight, he should emigrate and become a mujahir. If he can do neither one nor the other, he should keep his faith, even secretly if he has to, and try his best to pass it on at least to his descendants."
>
> (Kettani 1986 Page 3)

At this specific instance of his text Kettani lists the alternatives of (a) Jihad/mujahid, (b) the refugee/muhajir, (c) the silenced ortho-praxis/Muslim. The lessons of Kettani's text quoted above are found in the continuity of the discursive stream of jihad amongst the texts reviewed.

This is so because the defence of Islam is a fundamental part of the ortho-praxis of Islam and as such incumbent upon all Muslims to defend the din. Of serious importance is the need to respond on a daily basis to the incursions of the west upon the ortho-praxis of Islam in a minority position in the West.

The strategies presented by Kettani are all triggered into action whenever the minority Ummah are faced with a hostile state intent upon Muslim genocide, a la' Bosnia-Herzegovina 1994. But what are the strategies to respond to a kuffir state animated by Orientalist elites bent on eradicating the infection of the body politic? With a specific strategy of syncretic assimilation, which is just the glove, that masks the ever-present steel fist. How does the minority Ummah respond strategically to the West knowing fully well that the kuffir are always willing and able to resort to their minimalist "final solution"?

Kettani is disappointingly silent on this salient issue only offering the concept of Dar-al Muahadah/the Land of Treaty. Kettani states:

> "As there is a model for the Muslim state in the state established by the Prophet, there are also two models for Muslim minorities to follow; One is the model of a Muslim minority in Dar-al-Harb and the other is for the Muslim minority in a Dar-al-Muahadah."

> "The model of the Muslim community established by Muslim emigrants from Mecca to Abyssinia and organized by Jaafar Ibn Abi Talib, the cousin of the Prophet. In the first case, oppression led to warfare and eventually to the victory of truth over falsehood. In the second case, tolerance led to peaceful co-existence and exchange of ideas, making clear to everyone the truth from falsehood."

> (Kettani 1986 Page 259)

Kettani recognizes that the concept of the Treaty as the basis of peaceful co-existence between Muslim minorities and kuffir states is the strategic alternative afforded the Ummah by the Holy Quran. But he fails to enumerate upon the basis of this mutually agreed upon Treaty and its grounding in the Shar'ia of Islam.

The centrality of the need for fiqh that specifically applies to the realities of Muslim life in the West again comes to the fore, and on this Kettani is woefully silent. Moreover he fails to present that in the Sunnah of the Prophet Muhammad (uwbp) there is another body of praxis, which is the basis of the strategy of dealing with the kuffir state in the period of engagement, which ends with the acts of genocidal aggression against the Ummah. This period extends from the Call of Muhammad Abdullah to the Prophethood (uwbp) and ends with the Hejira of the Prophet (uwbp) and the rest of the Ummah to Medina. The Sunnah and Hadith of the Prophet (uwbp) during this period are then of prime importance in supplying answers to the questions that plague Muslim minorities in the West.

Kettani's work under review is then a panoramic view of the global realities of the minority Ummah of Islam rather than a treatise devoted to wrestling with the discursive realities of being Muslim minorities in Dar al Harb or even Dar al Muahadah. Finally, Kettani's typology on the genesis of Muslim minorities is of relevance to the focus of my work. Kettani's typology lists three scenarios, which resulted in the creation of Muslim minorities.

The first type is the result of the collapse of dar al Islam and the creation of a Muslim minority through deliberate anti-Islamic policies. Kettani states:

> "...the conquest of Muslim territories by non-Muslims, the result was that many Muslim majorities were brought under non-Muslim powers."

> "...when the occupation lasts long enough, the majority is transformed into a numerical minority because of large scale expulsion of Muslims, immigration of non-Muslims, and low rates of natural increase among Muslims owing to abnormally difficult conditions."

> (Kettani 1986 Page 4)

Kettani cites as examples of a Muslim minority as the product of state policy the minorities of Palestine, Thailand and Bosnia-Herzegovina.

The second type of Muslim minority is found in areas in which dar al Islam was dominant but Muslims were a minority. When dar al Islam was supplanted by a non-Islamic state the Muslims became in effect a minority.

The third type of Muslim minority is formed by the conversion of people to Islam in a kuffir state in effect creating a Muslim minority but more so the converted to Islam blend with a stream of immigrant Muslims from dar al Islam.

In this case Kettani cites the example of the Muslim minority of Sri Lanka. The realities of the Ummah of Trinidad and Tobago are not trapped by the matrices of the typology of minorities formulated by Kettani. In the case of Trinidad and Tobago blending of the immigrant stream and the converted to Islam has not taken place. The immigrant stream did not come from dar al Islam as they predominantly came from India then a colony of British colonialism whilst the recent converts are predominantly the descendants of West African slaves. In addition, the work of da'wa that accounted for the resurgence of Islam amongst the descendants of the West African slaves was not the work of the immigrant stream of the Ummah.

Da'wa amongst the Afro-Trinidadians that accounted for the resurgence of Islam outside of the immigrant stream was mainly the result of activities of the international Ummah, specifically from the United States, West Africa and the Middle East. The realities of the Ummah in Trinidad and Tobago therefore raises a possible fourth typology i.e. of the minority created by streams of Muslim immigration from Dar al Harb and streams of conversion dated after the end of Muslim immigration. Both streams are characterized by distinct agglomerations of persons of different races in both streams and the failure of the Ummah to transcend the divisions of race in the society. Trinidad and Tobago affords therefore very poignantly the evidence of the struggle of Islam against the racism that pervades a multi-racial postcolonial society of the periphery.

Answers must therefore be sought for the apparent and crippling inability of the discursive structures of Islam to supplant the discourse of racism that polices the post-colonial society of Trinidad and Tobago. The Ummah of Trinidad and Tobago affords then instances of the discursive struggles for hegemony between Islamic and Orientalist discourse and the spaces in which Islamic discourse has been breached resulting in varying instances of syncretism, assimilation, and in the perceptions of Islamic discourse, downright shirk.

In this struggle between Islamic and Orientalist discourse racism is then the most potent battering ram used on Islamic discourse towards perpetually ensuring that in Trinidad and Tobago there exists no Ummah as defined by the Holy Quran.

"Ye are the best Ummah evolved for mankind,
Forbidding what is wrong, And believing in God."

Sura 3:10

Faced with the perceptions of a hostile kuffir state any segment of the Muslim minority in Trinidad and Tobago has then to deal with the reality that a fragmented minority community is in fact even weaker when faced with a hostile kuffir state. With this realization uppermost in their minds the Muslim minority in Trinidad and Tobago has adopted various strategic responses to deal with this reality.

At this juncture of the work we would deal with the final review of this chapter, which delves into the project aimed at the Islamization of knowledge being carried out by Muslim social scientists that make up the Muslim minority of the United States of America. The articles that would be reviewed are products of this ongoing attempt of Muslim's living in the United States of America to create an ongoing process of the deconstruction of Western discourse, worldview, and epistemology. It is a process of discovery and creativity for ultimately the Western Muslim in a minority position has to work out his/her own strategies of survival as a Muslim minority in the West.

Mona Abul-Fadl in "Beyond Cultural Parodies and Parodizing Cultures: Shaping a Discourse" approaches the twin tasks of deconstruction and survival via the construct of contrasting epistemes which are, (a) an Oscillating Culture type and, (b) a Median Culture type.

Upon this construct she builds a structure devoted to deconstruction utilizing the tools of a contrasting episteme which are defined, conceptualised and modelled along a worldview which could only have arose out of the episteme she is deconstructing. Whereas Taha J. al `Alwa^ni^ in the article "Taqlid and Ijtihad" approaches the issue of deconstruction in a different manner insisting that the methodology of deconstruction must be built upon tools, constructs, concepts drawn from the Islamic worldview, discourse and re-tooled to do the job on Western discourse.

Both articles then indicate the intensity of debate going on within the Muslim minorities of the West towards grappling with the largely unresolved issue of the development of strategies of survival for the Muslim minorities especially in the West. The salient reality is that the strategies must be developed at the level of Islamic fiqh/jurisprudence. Thereby raising the issue of the creation of methodologies of fiqh of relevance to Muslim minorities of the West.

Abul Fadl's position is that the process commences at the level of deconstruction of Western thought, discourse, and worldview. Abul Fadl states:

> "It has been the practice for the dominant paradigm to set the terms of rational discourse and for the "other" to defer in reverence.... In this case the tables are turned and the dominant paradigm, which is secularist, is viewed critically through the lens of a re-emerging tawhi^di^ paradigm.
>
> The purpose is not to engage in a text of will or vision, but to lay the ground for a discourse which can accommodate a genuine diversity-in-dignity for all, and which would include Self and Other in a re-formed world of inter-relatedness developed through new categories and points of reference."

(Abul Fadl 1991 Pages 5—6)

Abul Fadl is therefore positing the tawhi^di^ paradigm as the vehicle, the discursive battering ram of deconstruction raising the question if the present dominant paradigm can in fact be re-constructed to embrace diversity in tolerance. In Abul Fadl's insistence that the process of re-construction is possible she was inevitably led to use the post-modernist debate as the beacon of hope for the ultimate success of the task of deconstruction/re-construction. Abul Fadl states:

> "The prevailing secularist culture identified with modernity and with historical Occident subverts morality to power and principles to expedience. Unchecked in its morbid dynamism, it has become a global threat as its influence spreads to englobe every other culture, and its voice rules."

(Abul Fadl 1991 Page 16)

Given the expression of the pathologies of the secularist Occident above, Abul Fadl states her concept of the contrasting episteme and the methodology articulated upon it. Abul Fadl states:

"This is where a Contrasting Episteme is advocated as an approach and a strategy for bridging cultures and for a dynamic of critical reflection and reconstruction. It is inspired by a hermeneutic of mutuality, which takes difference as a dialectic for convergence."

(Abul Fadl 1991 Pages 16-17)

It is all well and good for Abul Fadl to posit this "Contrasting Episteme" or the tawhi∧di∧ paradigm for in this she is not unique. All the non-white peoples of the periphery have always posited alternate worldviews but the white man remains singularly unique in the way he/she deals with diversity.

For wherever throughout the periphery they met contrasting epistemes they dealt with them through the final solution; genocide.

What is then preventing the white man from dealing with the tawhidi paradigm in the same manner whenever it rears its head as a contrasting episteme within the heartland of the white worldview?

On this Abul Fadl is silent for she did not carry the process of discursive deconstruction/reconstruction to its extreme extrapolation. Ethnic cleansing as the ultimate defence of a discourse under threat. Abul Fadl states:

"There are three major assumptions that condition this premise; (1) Present civilization is at a crossroads, as it must deal with the existing chasm between its material accomplishments and its moral failures. (2) It is not enough to critique the prevailing culture, but the challenge is to transform it; and (3) the source for meeting such a challenge cannot be reinvented from the debris from existent cultures, but must be sought in the transcendent."

(Abul Fadl 1991 Page 17)

Abul Fadl focuses on the "moral failures" of the West and the inabilities inherent in the dominant paradigm in attempting to create solutions based on the debris of "extant cultures". She insists therefore that the task then is not critique of the paradigm but to transform it. How? Abdul Fadl states:

"Two basic culture types are projected to take their distinct stance from an outlook and understanding of the fundamental categories of existence, man, nature and life...In the one case we encounter a culture mode that takes its bearings from a horizontal axis, while in the other, the bearings are projected onto a vertical axis. The dominant paradigm today has been shaped against the horizontal axis, whereas the tawhidi episteme, which is the subject of recall and recollection from the depths of a universal and generic human history, evokes the vertical axis."

(Abul Fadl 1991 Page 17)

Herein lies the antinomies of Abul Fadl's position as indicated above for the alternate/contrasting episteme is conceptualised via the discursive structures of the dominant paradigm. This inevitably leads in Abul Fadl's work to (a) the creation of discursive constructs, which are only comprehensible within a discursive netherworld, demilitarised zone in which space is in discursive hegemonic transition, and that is ideally the mind of Abul Fadl.
(b) As a result Abul Fadl situates the deconstruction/reconstruction of discourse within a discursive realm of ideational struggle for itself, in itself and by itself.

This is the major flaw in her construct of the tawhi^di^ paradigm for she does a major disfavour to the ortho-praxis of Islam by conceptualising struggle only on the basis of ideational conflict. Abul Fadl states:

"Modes of thought and apprehension are projected into their sociocultural and historical plane in terms of variants of an Oscillating Culture-type and of a Median Culture type."

(Abul Fadl 1991 Page 17)

Abul Fadl states that the Tawhi^di^ Episteme was a median culture for it consists of an ideal core as the "mainstay of both episteme and culture, and was ultimately rejected in practice". The concept of the "ideal core" then drives her "Contrasting Episteme" thereby resulting in her positing of discursive deconstruction/reconstruction at the ideational level for she is not dealing with a materialist grounded ortho-praxis for the attainment of Paradise/Sufism.

She has then fallen into the trap of the ever beckoning and beguiling Western discourse. For she still views her tawhi^di episteme through the white man's worldview, a most potentially fatal mistake to make when contending with the white man's discourse. Abul Fadl expresses her reality as follows:

"...Muslims, like many An/Other in the Third World, are ineluctably caught in a catch-up game. In some ways, they have ended up more confounded than their counterparts in the West, who have at least come to doubt some of the virtues of their own prodigy.

Untrammelled in their infatuated pursuit, they cannot venture to reflect upon the gains, or indeed, upon whether in the struggle for survival, selfhood itself has become a computable value worth its pain. The modern Muslim has more often than not turned himself/herself into a shadow chasing shadows in a breathless Monty Python shadow play."

(Abul Fadl 1991 Page 25)

Does Abul Fadl free herself of this shadow play through the discursive construct of the contrasting episteme? It is my contention that given the perceptual flaws of the construct it has in fact heightened the shadow play with potentially dangerous implications for the ortho-praxis of Islam in a minority position in the West.

But Abul Fadl has dared to contend and in this it is of most importance to the minority Ummah in the West.

For the flow of ideas, the un-relenting aim of deconstructing the West lies at the basis of the creation of fiqh of relevance to the Ummah of the West for it is only via fiqh conceptualised in and for the Ummah of the West can the ortho-praxis of Islam transcend the boundaries of discursive worldviews.

The article of Taha J. al `Alwani then flows out of the same mode i.e. the discursive deconstruction of Western discourse and by extension the development of Islamic fiqh for the Ummah of the West. Alwani states:

"Among these issues are the following;
(1) The presentation of the Islamic theory of knowledge and its most important elements, means, and devices, and the role of each.
(2) The formulation of an exact and precise definition of the relationship between revelation (wahy) and reason, for this will help Muslims solve many of the problems arising from the relationship of knowledge to religion, and of knowledge to practice. It will also

help us understand ijtihad from the perspective of reality, experience and practice.

(3) The development of an agreed upon system of argument and dialogue, respect and acceptance for differing opinions and results, and an understanding as to why this is essential if the scholars are to guide the Ummah's footsteps aright."

(Alwani 1991 Page 142)

Given the passage quoted above the question arises of what is an Islamic Theory of knowledge in the specific sense of what way is Alwani using the concept "theory"?

In the stream of the white man's post Enlightenment positivist, worldview, even in the nihilist worldview of the white man's post-structuralist thinkers as Foucault the views of theory clearly cannot be Islamized. Further it is my position that given the centrality of revelation in the Islamic worldview there can be no Islamic "Theory" of knowledge. And this is by far the most worrying aspect of the praxis of the Muslim's under review namely Abul Fadl and Alwani.

To Islamize the white man's epistemology, his discursive structures, his worldview takes for granted two things: (a) that there is a basis of congruency, which allows the white man's knowledge to be Islamized.

In fact there is no such congruency and in this the writers of dar ul Islam who indefatigably reject the Western paradigm are instinctively correct.

Both Abul Fadl and Alwani are beguiled by the viscosity of the white man's discourse in its perennial drive/quest for power/knowledge in mistaking this for congruency with alternate discourse.

(b) Secondly both Abul Fadl and Alwani in their beguiled state mistake the hegemony of the white man's discourse for inherent structures of superiority, which engendered hegemony.

In this they are Orientalist in their perceptions of themselves as Muslims. They view the white man's hegemony as progressing from, as the outcome of a worldview, which must be Islamized to ensure the resurgence of the Ummah of Islam. In this fatally flawed position they fail to perceive the white man's hegemony as a product of given, materialist relations of production and technology. For them hegemony arises out of a specific episteme, an ideational existence and reality which is inherently superior.

The ultimate threats of this position are that, (a) in its haste to Islamize the white man's knowledge the baby can be thrown out with the bath water, with the baby being Islam.

(b) The progenitors of this Islamized knowledge can fail to perceive, to deal with the steel fist that drives the white man's discourse.

For the white man's discourse would respond according to its historical antecedents when faced with the challenge of an alternate discourse. Maybe the strategy entails syncretism to the extent where the contradictions of the discursive structures of Islam and the West are simply defused. Alwani states:

> "It is to be hoped that the methodology for the Islamization of knowledge will benefit from the resulting definitions, clarifications, and organization of a discipline so that it can one day stand on a solid methodological foundation. Only if this present dream becomes a reality will it become possible for Muslim Social Scientists to study social phenomenon, with all the attendant diversity and complexity, with an Islamic framework and paradigm and then begin the process of rebuilding Islamic civilization on the basis of its own understanding of the social sciences."

> (Alwani 1991 Page 142)

The passage quoted above is replete with the effects of Orientalist self-immolation and the blinkers it places on people of the periphery. Alwani insists that Islamic civilization can only begin its resurgence based on this syncretic product of the process of the Islamization of the white man's knowledge. Alwani and Abul Fadl therefore offer up for consideration another parody of the periphery that is the Muslim social scientist. What specie of zebra this is can only be answered in the realm of the parodying of the periphery.

Muslim and social scientist are concepts that are mutually exclusive, more so the very concept of social science so eulogized by both Abul Fadl and `Alwa^ni^ is in the throes of discursive exhaustion in the white man's paradigm.

To hold, to grasp discursive concepts which are one step away from being discarded on the scrap heap of discursive exhaustion and in so doing grant them relevance and insights that their creators no longer afforded them is a cruel indication of our perpetual self contempt in the periphery. It is through another route that the Ummah of the West must create its fiqh so vital to the application of the ortho-praxis of Islam to the West. The lynchpin of this process is ijtihad as applied within the limits to action set by revelation.

For both Abul Fadl and Alwani have failed to appreciate that it is the centrality of revelation in the transmission of knowledge, which separates and ever constitutes contradiction between the white man's and Islamic discourse. And in this the twain shall never meet except through syncretism in which revelation is held within the bounds created by ideational delimited spaces as the concept of the "ideal core" and the "Islamic Theory of Knowledge".

Herein lies the most potent danger for the Ummah of the West, for in this agenda of generating an ortho-praxis responsive to the daily lives of the Ummah in the West, the discourse of the West can be afforded its most potent portal to sublimate the ortho-praxis of Islam in the West.

The Fiqh of Grand Ayatollah Sayyid Ali Sistani of Iraq states on the issue of a Muslim living in a non-Muslim land as follows:

> "A Muslim who is born and raised in a Muslim country where he consciously and subconsciously absorbs the laws, values and teachings of Islam, grows up into a young person who is aware of the customs of his religion, following its path and is led by guidance. On the other hand, a Muslim who is born, and brought up in a non-Muslim country demonstrates the influence of that environment very clearly in his thoughts, ideas, behaviour, values, and etiquette unless his Lord helps him. This un-Islamic influence is seen more in the second generation of those who have migrated to non-Muslim countries. This was the reason for Islam's view on at-ta'arrub ba'd al-hijra as reflected in many ahadith. At-ta'arrub ba'd al-hijra literally means 'becoming shorn of one's percepts of faith after migrating [to city],' and technically it means leaving an environment where you could follow Islam and moving to a place where you maybe prone to not following Islam. Such a migration is counted as one of the major sins."

Sistani is repeating Shi'i fiqh, which dismisses migration by a Muslim, or Muslims to a non-Islamic state and the loss of one's Islamic faith as an act of derision on par with shirk. How then do Muslims who find themselves in a minority position within a kuffir/kufr state handle this reality according to Sistani? Sistani states:

"It is haram to travel to non-Muslim countries in the East or the West if that journey causes loss of the faith of a Muslim, no matter whether the purpose of that journey is tourism, business, education, or residence of a temporary or permanent nature, etc."

"If an immigrant Muslim, residing in a non-Muslim country, knows that his stay in that country will lead to loss of faith or that of his children, it is wajib on him to return to one of the Muslim countries."

The threat of loss of faith of the Muslim and her/his children makes it a compulsory act to leave the kufr state for a Muslim state. What actions then constitute a loss of faith? Sistani states as follows:

"What do the jurists mean when they speak of, 'loss of faith'? It means either committing a forbidden act by indulging in minor and major sins like drinking intoxicant, adultery, eating forbidden meat or drinking najis (impure) drinks, etc. It also means abandoning the fulfilment of a compulsory act like neglecting salat, fasting, hajj, and other obligations."

Sistani does not even want to envisage apostasy as the direct result of the pressures of the non-or anti Islamic social order of the kuffir state and the impact on the Muslim who migrates to such state. The end result is a fiqh, which is of little relevance to Muslims in a minority position in kuffir states. It is a fiqh in denial for the Muslim minorities created specifically by North Atlantic colonial domination do exist and those of us who belong to the Ummah of the West especially have to deal with our din and the need to lead sustainable lives on a daily basis must now create the fiqh vital and relevant to our existence.

SUMMARY/CONCLUSION

That the minority Ummah of the West must produce fiqh to handle the ortho-praxis of Islam in the West is clearly a strategic prerogative. But the issue is the how of creating this fiqh so vital to the ortho-praxis of Islam in the West.

I have reviewed writers of Dar ul Islam who blatantly insist either that it is well nigh impossible to have an ortho-praxis of Islam in Dar ul Harb as Qutb or that Muslims outside of Dar ul Islam must incessantly and of necessity adopt militant stances of resistance against Dar ul Harb even to the point of Jihad and Shahid such as Mawdudi and Jameelah.

Underpinning both positions are rejectionist stances within dar ul Islam as Qutb, Mawdudi, and Jameelah who have turned their backs on the West spatially and perceptually. What then are the lessons from the rejectionist/militant engagement school of thought for Muslim minorities in the West?

This school evades the issue of whether rejectionist/militant engagement can be the basis for da'wa, as it is of secondary importance in the West given the existence of an environment that renders da'wa problematic in the West.

When you compare the rejectionist school with the Islamization of Knowledge school of thought you immediately discern the distance that separates their respective worldviews on the West. For the Islamization of Knowledge school da'wa is the be all and end all of their praxis but more so this school posits that it is the creation of Islamized knowledge from the West that is to free the Ummah from its fetters that renders it backward throughout the world.

The Islamized knowledge school rather than rejectionist in their stance seeks to re-create, to re-constitute Western knowledge in an Islamic mode. In doing this Muslims of this school have then to engage the West on a daily basis running the risk of perpetual encounter giving rise to syncretism.

The final school presented is the Shi'i who present yet another distinct path, for theirs is one based on a mix of strategic devices aimed at ensuring the integrity of space/s under the control of Shi'i Islamic discourse.

These devices span the gamut of human action from taqiyyah to martyrdom, all geared towards survival of Shi'i Islam. The strategic measures of Shi'i Islam are therefore supremely pragmatist as defined within the bounds set by revelation.

A central issue to all schools of thought reviewed is the question of ijtihad, more so to the Muslim minorities in the West the development of fiqh that responds to the ortho-praxis of Islam for Muslim minorities of the West is tied to the issue of ijtihad.

Shi'i Islamic ortho-praxis has developed in response to the growth of fiqh in response to specific realities encountered in the daily lives of the Ummah through time. In Sunni Islam ijtihad has become enclosed within the bounds of the debate on the innate perfection of the schools of fiqh already completed.

The question of and the consequent debate on the closure of the door of ijtihad rob the Sunni Ummah in the West of the flexibility of response afforded the Shi'i Ummah in the West.

The Sunni Ummah who maintain the traditional position on ijtihad are then locked into a mindset that can grow increasingly rejectionist and isolationist which increases the tendency to resort to ethnic traits and characteristics to create and replicate a community of distinct, identifiable boundaries distinct from non-Islamic society. In this development the universalising concepts of Islam are subverted and the ortho-praxis becomes particularized much to the detriment of the da'wa.

The potent lesson afforded by this journey through the texts is that for a Muslim in a minority position in the West how he/she relates to, deals with and interacts with the kuffir state on a daily basis is a grey area in the ortho-praxis of Islam.

The fiqh that renders the ortho-praxis current and relevant either remains unformulated or non-existent. The Muslim has then in the absence of current fiqh to navigate the minefield of daily existence in a kuffir state utilizing the Sunnah of the Prophet (uwbp) and a range of other measures from the fiqh of the four traditional schools of Sunni Islam or current Shi'i fiqh to the schools of thought some of which I reviewed to the practice of ijtihad on a personal level. Whatever mix the Muslim utilizes what it results in is a fragmented ortho-praxis that in its diversity is at its most potent weakness.

For in the absence of current fiqh the ortho-praxis is made even more accessible to the ravages of Western discourse and its range of depredations from syncretism/accommodation to ethnic cleansing. In turn Muslims of the West when faced with a perceptually hostile state have then the ability to respond via the range of strategic responses available without the influence of fiqh upon the decision to adopt a given strategic response available in the ortho-praxis.

The Muslim in the West can then respond to the perceptually hostile kuffir state by a gamut of responses from accomodationist/particularism to Jihad/Martyrdom. These decisions are ultimately made without the intervention of fiqh and the fuqaha that promulgate fiqh. The Muslims of the West until the promulgation of relevant fiqh are doomed to run the treadmill of kuffir history.

For every act of resistance to the challenge of the kuffir state is in fact a discontinuity, a break in the development of the Ummah. Because there is no consequent development of jurisprudence that records, interprets and rules upon the fitness of the previous strategies adopted in response to the kuffir state.

And in and by doing this precedents are extrapolated for future situations that would arise. In its absence, the Ummah continually reacts to the incursions of the West and in so doing relentlessly fractures itself from within in the game of catch-up survival; until it becomes so fractured and de-Islamized ripe for the picking.

Chapter 3

THE DISCOURSE OF
AL QAEDA

"To those champions who avowed the truth day and night, And wrote with their blood and sufferings these phrases.

The confrontation that we are calling for with the apostate regimes does not know Socratic debates, Platonic ideals, nor Aristotelian diplomacy. But it knows the dialogue of bullets, the ideals of assassination, bombing, and destruction, and the diplomacy of the cannon and machine-gun.

Islamic governments have never and will never be established through peaceful solutions and cooperative councils. They are established as they (always) have been by pen and gun

By word and bullet

By tongue and teeth.

(Al Qaeda Manual)

The discourse of the quotation is neither new nor unique to Islamic discourse especially anti-colonial Islamic discourse of Pakistan and Egypt. The line of the shahid begins the statement and sets the tone for jihad against the most potent enemy of Islam spawned by Jahiliyya: the munafikun, the apostate, the secular atheist. Jihad premised upon the praxis of the shahid is the means not only of engagement but also the assurance of victory. The governments of apostasy that rule over Dar ul Islam must now be engaged with militarily even to the point of plunging Dar ul Islam into Dar ul Harb. The call is then for Jihad to purge Dar ul Islam of the traits, tendency and manifestation of Jahiliyya.

> "Pledge, O Sister
> To the sister believer whose clothes the criminals have stripped off.
> To the sister believer whose hair the oppressors have shaved.
> To the sister believer who's body has been abused by the human dogs.
> To the sister believer whose
> Pledge, O Sister
> Covenant, O Sister to make their women widows and their children orphans
> Covenant, O Sister to make them desire death and hate appointments and prestige.
> Covenant, O Sister to slaughter them like lambs and let the Nile, al-Asi, and Euphrates rivers flow with their blood.
> Covenant, O Sister to be a pick of destruction for every godless and apostate regime.
> Covenant, O Sister to retaliate for you against every dog who touch you even with a bad word.
> (The covenant of the male shahid with Muslim women)
>
> (Al Qaeda Manual)

Shariah law excludes women and children with military engagement against the apostate. Given this exclusion it is then the duty of the male Muslim to protect, to avenge, to purge Dar ul Islam of Jahiliyya. The prime directive is then engagement with, the eradication of regimes that rule over Dar ul Islam that have turned their backs on the Din.

> "After the fall of our orthodox caliphates on March 3rd, 1924 and after expelling the colonialists, our Islamic nation was afflicted with apostate rulers who took over in the Moslem nation. These rulers turned out to be more infidel and criminal than the colonialists themselves. Moslems have endured all kinds of harm, oppression, and torture at their hands.

But they (the rulers) did not stop there; they started to fragment the essence of the Islamic nation by trying to eradicate its Moslem identity. Thus, they started spreading godless and atheistic views among the youth. We found some that claimed that socialism was from Islam, democracy was the (religious) council, and the prophet-God bless and keep him-propagandised communism.

Colonialism and its followers, the apostate rulers, then started to openly erect crusader centers, societies, and organizations like Masonic Lodges, Lions and Rotary Clubs, and foreign schools. They aimed at producing a wasted generation that pursued everything that is western and produced rulers, ministers, leaders, physicians, engineers, businessmen, politicians, journalists, and information specialists.

(The Al Qaeda Manual)

The discourse of Al Qaeda paraphrased with glimpses of its worldview afforded. It is a discourse that is solely focused on purging Dar ul Islam through military engagement of all that constitutes a threat to Islam. Islam in its minority position in the west is then irrelevant and in keeping with the discourse of Qutb an aberration. The prime directive is to purge Dar ul Islam of the hegemony of the apostate and the munafikun.

Military engagement with the west, in the west to the absolute detriment of the Muslims who live in the west is then acceptable collateral damage to Al Qaeda. The military strategies to purge Dar ul Islam of the apostate and the munafikun merits the destruction of the imperative to da'wa in the west, Muslims of the west now find themselves faced with a hostile, racist orientalist west and discourses of Dar ul Islam that see us only as aberrations, fitting evidence of the end result of Dar ul Islam falling under the hegemony of the apostate and munafikun.

"The young men returning to Allah realized that Islam is not just performing rituals but a complete system: Religion and government, worship and Jihad (holy war), ethics and dealing with people, and the Koran and the sword. The bitter situation that the nation has reached is a result of its divergence from Allah's course and his righteous law for all places and times. That (bitter situation) came about as a result of its children's love for the world, their loathing of death, and their abandonment of Jihad (holy war)."

(The Al Qaeda Manual)

Dar ul Islam has stumbled; has faltered for under the hegemony of the apostate and the munafikun the praxis of Jihad and the Shahid has been rejected. Secularism has attempted to separate Islam from government. Jihad is banished from worship and the Koran has been rendered weaponless, empty-handed. The linchpin of this abhorrent reality in Dar ul Islam has been the love of life, the fear of death and gagging of Jihad. This is all well and good for Dar ul Islam but how does this discourse ensure the survival and expansion of the Islamic Ummah in the west? It is a discourse that presents the most potent threat to Islam in a minority position in the west since the crusades.

"Importance of the Military Organization:

1. Removal of those personalities that block the call's path. All types of military and civilian intellectuals and thinkers for the state.
2. Proper utilization of the individuals' unused capabilities.
3. Precision in performing tasks, and using collective views on completing a job from all aspects, not just one.
4. Controlling the work and not fragmenting it or deviating from it.
5. Achieving long-term goals such as the establishment of an Islamic state and short-term goals such as operations against enemy individuals and sectors.
6. Establishing the conditions for possible confrontation with the repressive regimes and their persistence.
7. Achieving discipline in secrecy and through tasks."

(The Al Qaeda Manual)

All persons Muslims and non-Muslims that serve the regressive apostate regimes are military targets of the Jihad. The call is for total war in which civilians and Muslim are acceptable targets. In this call for total war non-Muslims are then targets that fall outside the pale of Islam, haram, agents of jahiliyya.

It is then open season on the agents of Jahiliyya and their progeny. Rabid intolerance and hate, which is now exhibiting racist and sexist discourse, borrowed from Orientalism thus Orientalism in reverse. In this discourse there is then no room for da'wa as there is space only for Islamic military expansion and hegemony. A discourse of denial which utterly fails to 'see' the realities of an unipolar globalised world in which there is no viable Dar ul Islam that can acquire the power to viably challenge the present unipolar hegemon: the USA.

> "It is my contribution toward paving the road that leads to majestic
> Allah and establishes a caliphate according to the prophecy."

> (Al Qaeda Manual)

The aim is then to create a block, a polar opposite to the US and the European Union. The means is then to re-establish the caliphate over Dar ul Islam, a looking back to the past hoping to replicate it in and for the future. A position bred by colonial domination of Dar ul Islam, a discourse linchpinned on the ontology of Orientalism that is the present spawn of Jahiliyya injected into the heart of the Ummah of the world.

The discourse is not unique in the flow of Islamic discourse as it is a reaction to European domination utilizing racist white ontology to liberate the Ummah of the yoke of colonial and neo-colonial oppression. The dream of the caliphate refuses to 'see' the present diversity of realities that impact the Ummah of the world. The heterogeneous strategic instances that Muslims must cope with the world over demands the creation of streams of discursive strategies devised to ensure da'wa and the replication of the praxis of Allah (swt) are never compromised.

The belief that there is but one discursive strategy for all Muslims is premised on the refusal to 'see' that as realities change over time the praxis of Allah (swt) is never rendered irrelevant. The praxis of humans is rendered irrelevant and unsustainable as long as it is not informed by revelation (wahy), which abrogates the limits of time and space.

> "The ruling to kill Americans and their allies-civilians and military-
> is an individual duty for every Muslim who can do it in any country
> in which it is possible to do it, in order to liberate the Al-Aqsa
> Mosque and the holy mosque from their grip, and in order for their

armies to move out of all the lends of Islam, defeated and unable to threaten any Muslim.

We-with God's help-call on every Muslim who believes in God and wishes to be rewarded, to comply with God's order to kill the Americans and plunder their money wherever and whenever they find it. We also call on Muslim ulema, leaders, youths, and soldiers to launch the raid on Satan's troops and the devil's supporters allying with them, and to displace those who are behind them so that they may learn a lesson."

(1998 Fatwa)

The Fatwa of 1998 simply then sums up the discourse of engagement, the total war of Jihad declared. The Fatwa of 1998 gave then ample warning to the enemies of Islam as constituted by the discourse of total war. Two specific incursions in New York City would be the basis of attacks on soft targets in the west that would include Madrid, Spain.

The invasion of Saddam's Iraq by the US and its coalition partners would now enable the launch on Saudi Arabia, the prime target. The soft underbelly of the dictatorship of the House of Saud is the dependence on non-Saudi personnel to run on a daily basis the energy economy of Saudi Arabia. A relentless military campaign that targets the foreign workers threatens to bring the Saudi energy economy to its knees and by extension escalating oil prices sparked off by the fears of the Saudi dictatorship's inability to assure the safety of its oil supply.

In a 1996 interview with NIDA ul Islam, Usamah Bin Ladin would in the course of the interview refer to the Saudi government as follows:

"At the same time that some of the leaders are engaging in the major kufr, which takes them out of the fold of Islam in broad daylight and in front of all the people,"

"and those who have taken visible and daring stances against the kufr activities which the regime is working."

"it is crucial to overlook many of the issues of bickering in order to unite our ranks so that we can repel the greater kufr."

(Nida ul Islam 1996)

For Bin Ladin, the House of Saud and its agents both military and civilian personnel are outside the pale of Islam. They are not even afforded the position of munafikun/hypocrites. They are anathema to Islam, outside the pale of Islam, they are kufr hence Islamic ethics, sensibilities and rules of engagement do not apply to them.

The discourse of Ibn Taymiyyah
Taymiyyah 1263 CE-1330CE is posited as the foremost proponent of the discourse of Jihad against the apostate, the munafikun. Taymiyyah is then cited as a major Islamic scholar in the Jihad against the greater kufr.

> "It has been established on the authority of the Qur'an, the Sunnah, and the Ijima (consensus) of the community, that those who depart from the law of Islam must be fought, even if they pronounce the two professions of faith."

> "There is, however, unanimity that is allowed to fight people for (not observing) unambiguous and generally recognized obligations and prohibitions, until they undertake to perform the explicitly prescribed prayers, to pay Zakaah, to fast during the month of Ramadan, to make pilgrimage to Makkah and to avoid what is prohibited, such as marrying women in spite of legal impediments, eating impure things, acting unlawfully against the lives and properties of Muslims and the like. If it is obligatory to take the initiative in fighting those people, as soon as the Prophet's (sallallaahu'alayhee-wasallam) summons with the reasons for which they are fought has reached them."

> (Ibn Taymiyyah)

Taymiyyah is then insisting that Jihad is obligatory in the fight against the kufr and the munafikun, the apostate. Those who are not Muslim and fail to pay the Jizya are then open to Jihad. Most of all Jihad is the means to police the Ummah to ensure it is protected from the infection of apostasy, backsliding and hypocrisy.

"The most serious type of obligatory Jihad is the one against the unbelievers and against those who refuse to abide by certain prescriptions of the Sharee'ah, like those who refuse to pay Zakaah, the khawaarij and the like. This Jihad is obligatory if it is carried out on our initiative and also if it is waged as defence. If we take the initiative, it is a collective duty (Fard kifayah), (which means that if it is fulfilled by a sufficient number (of Muslims) the obligation lapses for all others and the merit goes to those who have fulfilled it."

(Ibn Taymiyyah)

Jihad against the apostate, the greater kufr, is then obligatory upon the entire Ummah. Those who do not wage war physically are obligated to support the male elite that does so and the cause of Jihad. Hence the obligation to support the families of the shahid and the erection and maintenance of the walls of the Shahids and the burial grounds of the Shahids.

"The assistance, which is obligatory both for the regular professional army and for others, must be given, according to everybody's possibilities, either in person, by fighting on foot or on horseback, or through financial contributions, be they small or large.
So the latter (form of Jihad) consists in defence of the religion, of things that are inviolable, and of lives. Therefore it is fighting out of necessity. The former (type of Jihad), however, is voluntary fighting in order to propagate the religion, to make it triumph and to intimidate the enemy, such as was the case with the expedition to Tabrook and the like."

(Ibn Taymiyyah)

Jihad in defence of Islam against both the assault of the kufr and the apostate, munafikun is then compulsory an obligation upon all Muslims. Failure to abide by such an obligation is then shirk.

"Now, this form of punishment (i.e. jihad) must be administered to rebellious people. As for inhabitants of the territory of Islam who are not rebellious (but refuse to carry out religious duties), they must be forced to carry out their obligations such as the five fundamental duties of Islam and others like the delivering of trusts to their owners and the preserving of covenants in social relations."

(Ibn Taymiyyah)

Taymiyyah does not see the Ummah in a minority position outside of Dar ul Islam. The injunction to Jihad against the apostate, the munafikun, the greater kufr only applies to Dar ul Islam. The discourse of the Jihad against the greater kufr in the last decade of the 20th century and the early 21st century has then outstripped the geographic limitations as conceptualised by Ibn Taymiyyah. Globalisation has then facilitated the desire to strike at the kufr outside Dar ul Islam.

The brutality of the Jihad against the greater kufr is summed up in the slaughter of Muslims in the Darfur region of Sudan.

"The attack took place in at dawn of September 2003 when many Janjawid arrived on camels, horses and by cars. Some Arab women, on donkeys and on camels accompanied them. The women took part in the looting. I was sleeping when the attack took place. I was taken away by the attackers in khaki and in civilian clothes, along with dozens of other girls, and had to walk for three hours. During the day, we were beaten up and the Janjawid they told us: 'you, the black women, we will exterminate you; you have no God.' We were taken to a place in the bush where the Janjawid raped us, several times at night. For three days, we did not receive food and almost no water. After three days, the Janjawid had to move to another place and set us free. They told us: 'next time we come, we will exterminate you all, we will not even leave a child alive.'"

(Amnesty International)

"The attack took place at 6am on Sunday 29th June and was carried out by both Janjawid and the government, arriving on camels, horses and by cars-some 150 men in khaki in all. Two Antonov planes took part in the attack. Some 65 men were praying at the mosque. The horses, camels and cars surrounded the mosque and the shooting started. All the men in the mosque were killed."

(Amnesty International)

> "we don't know why the government burns our mosques and kills
> our imams" said Imam Abdullah, sixty five, of Janaza Kudumi. "Our
> Islam is good, we pray all the time, we read the Qoran all the time."
> "The government wants to kill all African people, Muslim or not
> Muslim, so as to put Arabs in their places," said Imam Abdullah.
> "They are not good Muslims".

(Human Rights Watch Vol. 16 No 6 (A))

In the Darfur region of the Sudan, Muslims who speak Arabic and are
rooted in the nomadic pastoralist culture/worldview of the arid/semiarid
spaces of northern Sudan are practising genocide and ethnic cleansing against
Muslims of Darfur who do not speak Arabic, are not nomads and pastoralists
but farmers, who predominantly practice the tenets of the Tajaniyya Sufi
Order. In a political order in which hegemony is exercised by power groupings
drawn from Muslims of the Arab cultural experience but moreso by groupings
who have embraced the discourse of the Jihad against the greater kufr the
Muslims of Darfur by their rebellion against racist hegemony have now
earned the wrath of the Arab racist hegemony of Sudan.

> "It was 2.30pm, time for prayers. The Janjaweed went in, on foot
> and on horseback, and killed ten people including the Imam, Yahya
> Gabat. Then they turned and started shooting in the market. The
> bullets were falling like rain and they were shouting: 'kill the Nuba!
> Kill the Nuba!' they killed my seventy-five-year old aunt, Kaniya
> Hassan, because she refused to let them take her sheep and goats."

(Human Rights Watch Vol. 16 No. 6(A))

The discourse of Arab racist hegemony would enter public discourse in
1987 with the appearance of a grouping of Darfur Arabs named the Arab
Gathering. The Arab Gathering would articulate a discourse of Arab hegemony premised upon inherent Arab superiority and the call for Arab hegemony in Darfur in light of the inherent superiority by the Arab and the refusal
of the non-Arabs of Darfur to bend to the desire for Arab hegemony.

The Islam of the non-Arab of Darfur had then to be problematised, to be
declared less than a true Islam, an Islam of the Arab, Orientalism in reverse.
The Arab militia-the Janjawid/Janjaweed armed by the present government of

Sudan which is made up of adherents to the discourse of the jihad against the greater kufr is then the instrument to purge from Darfur the apostate, the munafikun, the practitioners of a corrupted Islam worthy of Jihad towards its extinction from Dar ul Islam in Sudan. The kufr of the south of Sudan who dares to oppose the hegemony of Arab Islam have felt the barbarity of the Jihad of genocide unleashed by the Jihad against the kufr. By 2003 it was the turn of non-Arab Muslims of Darfur who dared to challenge the hegemony of Arab Islam to feel the force of the brutality of the Jihad against the greater kufr: apostasy.

The lesson of Darfur to the west and it is a lesson Muslims opposed to the Jihad of the greater kufr have long known is that adherents to the discourse of war against apostasy are willing to relentlessly flout one of the major pillars of Islamic ethics and praxis. All Muslims are prohibited from the murder of fellow Muslims. To do so is to place a Muslim outside the pale of Islam. The discourse of war against apostasy seeks to evade this prohibition by insisting that Muslims targeted are in fact apostates, hypocrites (munafikun), Muslims who are complicitious with the kufr. Muslims who then fail to stand as Shahids in the jihad against the greater kufr are then by their failure complicitious with the greater kufr, kufr or both.

The practitioners of Jihad against the greater kufr willingly and deliberately murder fellow Muslims utilising a discursive construct very much similar to that utilized by the extremist Marxist-Leninist guerrilla groups such as the Japanese Red Army, the Bader-Meinhof Gang, the Red Army Brigade of Italy, and groups in Greece during the late 1970's and early 1980's. In the history of Islam they are in fact of the lineage of the Kharijites but with a distinct discursive nature that flows from western extremist political discourse.

To murder fellow Muslims means in fact and in their praxis there is a penchant and predilection for demonstrative brutality against the unbelievers. Unbelievers, polytheists are viewed as less than human, a lower order of humans fit to be slaughtered for the ultimate hegemony of Islam over the world. The two attacks on the World Trade Center of New York, the Bali bombing and the Madrid bombing must be juxtaposed against the slaughter of Muslims in Iraq, Pakistan and Saudi Arabia for persons to realise that the praxis of the Jihad against the greater kufr is that of the Dajjal. It has nothing to do with civilization and the cultivation of a praxis of submission to the will of Allah (swt), that presents a discourse of the All Knowing that is premised upon the desire for hegemony, blood letting, exclusion devoid of dynamism and the moral imperatives as revealed in the Quran.

A discourse hinged on exoteric praxis, which disregards morel regeneration, moral imperatives and da'wa. It is a discourse that purports that it is Allah (swt) centered but in practice it focuses only on ritual and repetition as the expression of faith/din whilst leaving the pursuit of desire within a world-view very much akin to atheistic, secular worldview of the west. The discourse of Jihad against the greater kufr is then willing to assault the apostate, the munafikun but it would plant, produce and trans-ship illicit drugs for the purpose of waging jihad. The adherents of the war against the greater kufr see no moral conflict, no failing to exploit the weak, the poor, the infirm and women. They see no moral failing in a social order in the name of Islam that denies Muslims the opportunities to realise their fullest potential as Muslims.

Moreover, they refuse to 'see' that the Quran is rooted in a body of revealed moral imperatives that form the basis of, the foundation of Islam. Islam is then first a moral order of submission to the will of Allah (swt). A moral order, which insists on behavioural change and is the basis of a cognitive order that is the Islamic worldview. Muslims must then articulate and embody this Islamic worldview, this Islamic moral order, this Islamic cognitive order. When as Muslims aggregated as the Ummah we fail to abide by the Islamic worldview, to exhibit and articulate Islamic behaviour patterns, choices and desire, we fall short and by so doing aberrations arise that threaten the very existence of the Ummah. The dajjal in our midst Al Qaeda and others of the same ilk is the direct result of the failure of Muslims the world over to walk away from racism, elitism, hate, greed, oppression of the poor, the weak, the infirm, and women. The Dajjal conjured up by Muslims exists only to wage war on Muslims.

AL QAEDA IN TRINIDAD AND TOBAGO

The attempted coup d'etat by the Jamaat al Muslimeen on the 27th July 1990 has identified this grouping as the primary group under suspicion in Trinidad and Tobago as being adherents to the discourse of war against the greater kufr. The Imam of the Jamaat al Muslimeen, Yasin Abu Bakr, and the frontline leadership of the Muslimeen do not subscribe to the said discourse. Members of the Muslimeen frontline leadership who do subscribe to the said discourse have in fact left the Muslimeen and formed their own organisations both nationally and internationally. Yasin Abu Bakr has never indicated by his praxis a predilection to be influenced by the discourse of the war against the greater kufr.

In fact two signal aspects of the praxis of Imam Yasin Abu Bakr over the years indicate a praxis that is at odds with that of Al Qaeda and the Taliban. These are (a) the practise of justice for women within the ranks of the Jamaat al Muslimeen. Women are afforded full opportunity for their development as Muslims within the Muslimeen. Women are not locked within purdah denied educational opportunities, and pinned in a hegemony of the male. It is a commonly heard complaint among the males of the Muslimeen that the Imam is regularly sympathetic to the cause of the woman in disputes with their husbands within the membership of the Muslimeen.

(b) Yasin Abu Bakr has always engaged with the political structure of Trinbago in a bid to increase the level and frequency of opportunities that are available to members of the Muslimeen. Abu Bakr has always insisted that with a membership drawn from the urban working poor and underclass the needs of the membership of the Muslimeen must also be addressed politically. The Muslimeen have always insisted that the basis of its da'wa is addressing the ills of the Trinbagonian social order and devising Islamic solutions.

The attempted coup d'etat irretrievably harmed and retarded the development of the Muslimeen towards being a premier Islamic institution in Trinbago in the decade of the 1990's and the twenty-first century. In fact the reality is that those who make war against the greater kufr neither agreed with nor accepted the need for the jihad of July 27th 1990. There are various reasons for this: (a) the sympathizers of the said war in Trinbago were party to the war of the NAR government with the Muslimeen over the land at No.1 Mucurapo Road and the Muslimeen's war on the drug blocks. (b) The agents of the war against the greater kufr insisted to the Muslimeen that the jihad cannot and wouldn't serve the interests against the greater kufr. They insisted to the Muslimeen that there must be peace with the NAR government even to the detriment of the Muslimeen. Leading to July 1990 the Muslimeen was therefore alone in its battle with the NAR government and sought alliances with forces that would enable its jihad given the reality that it stood alone, even kufr forces.

The Ummah in Trinbago in 1990 and today remains deeply divided on the basis of race: Afro-Trinbagonian vs Indo-Trinbagonian. The Indo-Trinbagonian Muslim has tied Islam to a genetic identity that must be maintained by copulation and reproduction within a specific genetic structure. South Asian genes must not be mixed with African, mixed, etc. for this endangers the South Asian genetic identity with miscegenation, douglarisation. The impetus has been then not to practice da'wa to the African population of Trinbago. The ultimate fear is then of the Indo-Trinbagonian women marrying Afro-Trinbagonian males thereby producing bi-racial, mixed race offspring.

To maintain its genetic identity Indo Trinbagonian Muslims have then bought into the discourse of racist hegemony and have always looked to India and now Pakistan rather than the Middle East for waves of discursive structures to bolster their racist hegemonist worldview within Islam, the most potent example of the greater kufr in the west. First came the Ahmadiyya who created the trojan horse of their da'wa of shirk, the Trinidad Muslim League (TML) and thereafter came the discourse of the war against the greater kufr. From the late 1970's Indian Islam have been sending successive waves of their sons to Pakistan for training in the madrassas of the mujahidun of the war against the greater kufr. Pakistani's have been coming to Trinbago marrying Indo-Trinbagonian Muslim women and settling in Trinbago.

The sympathizers and the agents of the war against the greater kufr have swept over Indian Islam and have steadfastly moved to control organisations and masjids within Indian Islam. They have settled and dominated specific geographic areas under the control of Indian Islam thereby configuring the landscape and sensibilities of Indian Islam. The racist hegemonist hate has heightened and in areas of central and south Trinidad one swears that one is in Taliban controlled Afghanistan and Pakistan rather than in Trinidad which is positioned in the belly of the kufr beast. The denial of a twisted and distorted Islam that sees the world through racist hegemonist hate and exclusion is bent on creating spaces that exclude Afro-Trinbagonians especially Muslims.

This is then the fertile ground for Al Qaeda in Trinbago as they are present and active here. Why then is Al Qaeda in Trinbago? For one because of a welcoming Indian Islam they are given presence, succour and operational opportunity. Secondly, in the war against the greater kufr Trinidad is the largest single supplier of LNG via tankers to the USA from Atlantic LNG at Point Fortin, Trinidad. LNG tankers from Trinidad regularly traverse Boston Harbour to offload cargoes as the Distrigas LNG re-gasification terminal at Everett, Massachusetts, USA. To strike at the USA outside of the USA, the opportunity to strike at the USA in Boston Harbor is afforded by LNG manufactured in Trinidad.

Thirdly and perhaps the most important reason why they are in Trinbago is Trinbago's strategic position in the illicit drug trade to Europe. Al Qaeda in Trinbago is heavily involved in the trans-shipment of cocaine and heroin from Venezuela to Trinbago, to Europe. Al Qaeda cells present in Colombia, Venezuela and Guyana interact with those in Trinbago towards ensuring a sustainable trafficking network to Europe. Al Qaeda and its local agents and sympathisers import, wholesale and retail illicit drugs arms and ammunition in Trinbago with their main target being the Afro-Trinbagonian population. The mujahidun of the war against the greater kufr is so well integrated into the narco-trafficking economy that they now have allies and minions within both major political parties, the PNM and the UNC and have presence in the present PNM cabinet and the last two UNC cabinets.

The most alarming development is the rapid integration of Guyana into the drug and arms trafficking structures of Al Qaeda. Guyana is now a major offshore production center for the Columbian drug networks. Coca paste is being imported into Guyana for the production of cocaine hydrochloride and then exported to Caribbean destinations for delivery to Europe and the USA. Al Qaeda has a presence in this Guyana reality and is seeking to increase its take from this operation towards ensuring the financial viability of its network in Trinbago and Guyana, the influence it can buy with the cash resources it commands and the financial contributions the Trinbagonian operations make the global networks.

The Madrid bombings of 2004 were directly linked to the reality that Spain is the largest single importer of illicit drugs from Latin America trafficked through the Caribbean. The Spanish financial structure is fully integrated into the Latin American illicit drug networks hence the ease with which a mujahidun cell involved in the illicit drug trade planned and executed the Madrid bombings with impunity. The lesson of the Madrid bombings is the price a society targeted for war against the greater kufr and will pay given its complicity with the illicit drug trade.

The mujahidun of this war are fully integrated into the illicit drug trade of the world and would effectively use the opportunities and finances afforded by this trade to wage the war against the greater kufr. Shukrijumah's presence in Trinbago and Guyana was not then the product of happenstance. Shukrijumah visited Trinbago fully clothed and was given succour, mobility and organizational effectiveness by Indian Islam. This is but a simple indication of the structures that exist and the potential to strike. At best the presence can be one solely charged with reaping the rewards of illicit drugs and arms trafficking and seeking to deepen its presence within and ties to the political order. At worst the catastrophic potential can be triggered and a strike sets in train a dynamic that irretrievably results in a conflagration involving the US.

Whatever the outcome the Ummah of Trinbago is in acute crisis for the discourse of Indian racist hegemony has now set in train the march towards a catastrophic confrontation with the hegemon of the present globalized world capitalist order: the USA. Given the strategic importance of Trinbago's gas resources to the US energy market and the integration of the mujahidun of the war against the greater kufr into the illicit drug trade engagement with, towards the destruction of the mujahid cell in Trinbago is destined to trigger a confrontation with the USA in which the social order and stability of Trinbago would be the victim and the Ummah in Trinbago would be further rent asunder for it was the turn of the Muslimeen in 1990 and thereafter. The early 21st century is now the turn of Indian Islam an aberration that can only invite the wrath of Allah (swt).

> "And from among you there should be a party who invite to good and enjoin what is right and forbid the wrong, and these it is shall be successful."
>
> (Quran Sura 111:104)

> "And were it not for Allah's repelling some men with others, the earth would certainly be in a state of disorder; but Allah is Gracious to the creatures."
>
> (Quran Sura 11:251)

> "O, you who believe! Be maintainers of justice, bearers of witness of Allah's sake, though it may be against your own selves or (your) parents or near relatives, if he be rich or poor, Allah is nearer to them both in compassion, therefore do not follow (your) low desires, lest you deviate; and if you swerve or turn aside, then surely Allah is aware of what you do."
>
> (Quran Sura 4:135)

"Or do you think that you would enter the garden while yet the state of those who have passed away before you has not come upon you; distress and affliction befell them and they were shaken violently, so that the Apostle and those who believed with him said: When will the help of Allah come? Now surely the help of Allah is nigh."

(Quran Sura 2:214)

THE LETTER OF ABU MUSAB al-ZARQAWI

In February 2004 the Coalition Provisional Authority of Iraq published what is supposedly a letter written by al-Zarqawi to Al Qaeda. It is not my intention to enter into any debate on the issue of al-Zarqawi and the bona fide of the said letter. The discourse of the said letter is deconstructed; its discursive constructs are laid bare to reveal their discursive origin and pedigree.

"As you know, God favoured the nation with jihad on his behalf in the land of Mesopotamia. It is known to you that the arena here is not like the rest. It has positive elements not found in others, and it also has negative elements not found in others. Among the greatest positive elements of this arena is that it is jihad in the Arab heartland. It is a stone's throw from the two Holy Precincts and the al-Aqsa. We know from God's religion that the true, decisive battle between infidelity and Islam is in this land, i.e. in Syria and its surroundings. Therefore, we must spare no effort and strive urgently to establish a foothold in this land."

The American led invasion and occupation of Iraq has now created the opportunity for jihad against the greater kufr in a second tier geographical space as it borders the two Holy Precincts and al-Aqsa. Engagement with the greater kufr in Iraq is simply then a prelude to the ultimate task of liberating the two Holy Precincts from the grasp of the greater kufr. Jihad in Iraq is then a staging ground, a preamble to the primary ultimate jihad, the liberation of the Holy Precincts.

"I say, having sought help from God, that the Americans; as you know well, entered Iraq on a contractual basis and to create the state of Greater Israel from the Nile to the Euphrates an that this

Zionized American Administration believes that accelerating the creation of the State of Israel will accelerate the emergence of the Messiah. It came to Iraq with all its people, pride, and haughtiness toward God and his prophet."

The American led coalition invaded and occupied Iraq not to end a dictatorship, not to liberate Iraq, not to end the threat of weapons of mass destruction but to expand and create the state of Greater Israel. The American led invasion and occupation of Iraq is for the specific purpose to accelerate the Armageddon between Israel and Islam out of which the resurgent, second coming of the Christian Messiah would be made manifest. The American led invasion and occupation of Iraq is then but another manifestation of the greater kufr, the affront to Allah (swt) and his prophet (uwbp).

"This forced the Americans to conclude a deal with the Shi'a, the most evil of mankind. The deal was concluded on the Shi'a would get two-thirds of the booty for having stood in the ranks of the Crusaders against the mujahidun."

The Shi'a of Iraq has in fact stood with thee American led invaders and occupiers rather than against them. The Shi'a have done so because the Shi'a are hypocrites, munafikun, outside the pale of Islam and an enemy of the jihad against the greater kufr.

"the insurmountable obstacle, the lurking snake, the crafty and malicious scorpion, the spying enemy, and the penetrating venom. We here are entering a battle on two levels. One evident and open, is with an attacking enemy and patent infidelity, a difficult, fierce battle with a crafty enemy who wears the garb of a friend, manifests agreement, and calls for comradeship, but harbors ill will and twists up peaks and crests.

The unhurried observer and inquiring onlooker will realize that Shi'ism is the looming danger and the true challenge.

History's message is validated by the testimony of the current situation, which informs most clearly that Shi'ism is a religion that has nothing in common with Islam except in the way that Jews have something in common with Christians under the banner of the

People of the Book. These are people who added to their infidelity and augmented their atheism with political cunning and a feverish effort to seize upon the crisis of governance and the balance and the balance of power in the state, whose features they are trying to draw and whose new lines they are trying to establish through their political banners and organizations in cooperation with their hidden allies the Americans."

In Iraq where the Shi'a is the dominant majority of the population the discourse of Shi'a Islam as being of the greater kufr is the basis for a civil war premised on racist genocide. The discourse in fact sees more enemies within Islam than outside and would in fact be the basis for repeated engagement with the kuffir against perceived enemies within the pale of Islam. The discourse of vitriolic genocidal hatred against Shi'a Islam means in fact that the jihad against the greater kufr is willing, able and has in fact colluded with the kuffir to limit and hinder the creation of an Iraq under the control of the Shi'a.

"As the days pass, their hopes are growing that they establish a Shi'a state stretching from Iran through Iraq, Syria and Lebanon and ending in the cardboard kingdom of the Gulf."

This then is the strategic imperative of the jihad against the greater kufr, to prevent, to ensure that this Shi'a geo-political continuum is never attained. And to ensure this the jihad against the grater kufr has worked assiduously with the kufr to block its realization. That is why an Iran armed with nuclear weapons is now a major anathema of the kufr and its handmaiden: Al Qaeda.

"The American army has begun to disappear from some cities, and its presence is rare. An Iraqi army has begun to take its place, and this is the real problem that we face, since our combat against the Americans is something easy. The enemy is apparent, his back is exposed, and he does not know the land or the current situation of the mujahidin because his intelligence information is weak.
This enemy, made up of the Shi'a filled with Sunni agents, is the real danger that we face, for it is our fellow countrymen, who know us inside and out. They are more cunning than their Crusade masters, and they have begun, as I have said, to try to take control of the security situation in Iraq.

I believe, and God knows best, that the worst will not come to pass until most of the American army is in the rear lines and the secret Shi'i army and its military brigades are fighting as its proxy. They are infiltrating like snakes to reign over the army and police apparatus, which is the strike force and iron fist in our Third World, and to take complete control over the economy like their tutors the Jews."

The primary target is then the Shi'a dominated police and army for they are the most potent threat against the jihad against the greater kufr. The Shi'a have then to be assaulted given the potent threat they are to the jihad against the grater kufr.

"There is no doubt that the space in which we can move has begun to shrink and that the grip around the throats of the mujahidin has begun to tighten. With the deployment of soldiers and police the future has become frightening."

The clear and present danger posed to the jihad against the grater kufr must necessitate a specific strategy to engagement with Shia Islam in Iraq.

"If we succeed in dragging them into the arena of sectarian war, it will become possible to awaken the inattentive Sunnis as they feel imminent danger and annihilating death at the hands of those Sabeans."

"I come back and again say that the only solution is for us to strike the religious, military, and other cadres among the Shi'a with blow after blow until they bend to the Sunnis. Some one may say that, in this matter, we are being hasty and rash and leading the nation into a battle for which it is not ready, that will be revolting and in which blood will be spilled. This is exactly what we want, since right and wrong no longer have any place in our current situation. The Shia has destroyed all those balances. God's religion is more precious that lives and souls when the overwhelming majority stands in the ranks of truth, there has to be a sacrifice for this religion. Let blood be spilled, and we will soothe and speed those who are good to their paradise. Those who, unlike them are evil, we will be delivered from

them, since by God, God's religion is more precious than anything
and has priority over lives, wealth and children."

The strategy is then to assault the Shi'a in Iraq with the hope of precipitating a sectarian war that would suck the Sunni majority into the final solution
of once or for all breaking the back of the Shi'a heresy in Islam, a discourse
and a military strategy that serves the geo-political imperatives of the kufr.
Further compelling evidence that the jihad against the greater kufr serves the
interests of the kufr and constitutes the most potent threat to Islam in the
early twenty first century. The jihad against the greater kufr is the spawn of the
infidel, the handmaiden of the kufr.

The discourse of the Shia enunciated in the said letter is by no means a
deviation in Sunni Islamic discourse. A fatwa on Sunni and Sheeahs by Shaykh
Ibn'Uthaymeen al-Aqalliyaat al-Muslimah states:

> "There are many differences between the Sunni and Shee'ah.
> However, some of the most important are as follows Ahlus-Sunnah
> are compassionate and merciful towards the Companions of the
> Prophet. It is well known, however, that the group the questioner
> mentioned slanders, defames and maligns the Companions. They
> consider them to be sinful and impious and they believe that they
> left Islam after the death of the Prophet (sal-Allaahu'alayhe wa sal-
> lam). In fact, their slandering of the Companions is not only slander
> and defamation of them, but rather it is slander and defamation of
> the Companions, the Messenger of Allah (sal-Allaahu'alayhe wa sal-
> lam) the religion of Islaam, and it is also slander and defamation of
> Allaah's wisdom."

The fatwa pronounces the Shia as shirk, anathema to Islam. Military action
and sectarian warfare are then perfectly justified against the Shia wherever they
are found, Iraq, India, Pakistan and Lebanon. The so-called al-Zarqawi letter
then flows with the discourse of Saudi Islam. This discourse constitutes the
military engagement of the jihad against the greater kufr. To decry the methodology of military engagement is then to do so for strategic imperatives rather
than conviction. For it is a discourse driven by the desire for hegemony, for geo-
political dominance realized through a worldview of anathema and exclusion.
In its formulation it is the offspring of dualist exclusion and consequently it

reeks of the hate borne out of a worldview premised on a totality. In this, the discourse is the product of western colonial discourse rather than Islamic discourse rooted in the Quran. Western colonial discourse has then implanted within the Ummah discursive hybrids, which are now blossoming, threatening the very sustainability of the Ummah Wasat.

> "Jihad here unfortunately mines planted, rockets launched, and mortars shelling from afar. The Iraqi brothers still prefer safety and returning to the arms of their wives, where nothing frightens them. Sometimes the groups have boasted among themselves that not one of them has been killed or captured. We have told them in our many sessions with them that safety and victory are incompatible, that the tree of triumph and empowerment cannot grow tall and lofty without blood and defiance of death, that the nation cannot live without the aroma of martyrdom and the perfume of fragrant blood spilled on behalf of God, and that cannot awaken from their stupor unless talk of martyrdom and martyrs fills their days and nights."

This is the discourse of jihad taken to its end, its terminus in blood lust in which Allah (swt) is portrayed as the god of blood lust in keeping with the Christian god of the crusades, the god of the Nazis and that of the Serbs in Bosnia. This is then the consummate discourse of shirk bequeathed to the Ummah Wasat of the early 21st century and the one that is most appealing to the Ummah as they fail to grasp the reality that this discourse of jihad is rooted in western discourse, epistemology and ontology rather than the discourse of the Quran. It is then clearly apparent that in the early 21st century it is the duty, the call, the jihad of Muslims of the west to deconstruct, to expose the reality that the discourse of the jihad against the greater kufr is the product of western colonial hegemony. Al Qaeda is the dajjal spawned in the discourse of the west to tear asunder the fabric of the Ummah Wasat.

> "This is our path, and we have made it clear. If you are with us on it, if you adopt it as a program and road, and if you are convinced of the idea of fighting the sects of apostasy, we will be your readied soldiers, working under your banner, complying with your orders, and indeed swearing fealty to you publicly and in the news media, vex-

ing the infidels and gladdening those who preach the oneness of God."

The primary target of the jihad is the sects of apostasy which means that the party of Saud, the ruling elite of Saudi Arabia of the bloodline of Saud is the mother of all apostates. All other attacks whether in the US, Spain, Pakistan, Afghanistan and Iraq were executed to serve the terminal strategy i.e. the downfall of the party of Saud in Saudi Arabia. In this reality the carrion have come home to roost. A letter supposedly from the Abu Hafs al-Masri Brigades states:

> "A word for the foolish Bush. We know that you live in the worst days of your life in fear of death squads, which spoilt your world, and we are very keen that you do not lose in the forthcoming elections as we know very well that any big attack can bring down your government and this is what we do not want. We cannot get anyone who is more foolish that you, who uses force instead of wisdom and diplomacy. Your stupidity and religious extremism is what we want as our people will not awaken from their deep sleep except when there is an enemy."

The historical reality is that the jihad against the greater kufr was born out of the sectarian wars against Shi'a Islam accelerated after the Iranian Islamic Revolution of 1979. Al Qaeda is but one name for an agglomeration of Sunni Muslims who formed various alliances with the west to at minimum halt the spread of the Iranian Islamic Revolution or at best to destroy the said Islamic Revolution.

The Lebanese civil war of the early 1970's would set the stage for the creation of power relations that would be a catalyst towards radically altering the power relations of Lebanon in which the Shi'a of Lebanon were literally at the bottom of the Lebanese social order in spite of the telling proportion of the Lebanese population they constituted. As in Iraq the Shi'a were condemned to a futile life of poverty, ignorance and underdevelopment because of sectarian violence and oppression meted out by the Sunni Muslims, the Christians and the Druze in Lebanon. In Iraq the majority Shia were placed under the hegemony of the Sunni Muslims and then secular Baathists preaching a sterile, atheist Arab socialism which culminated in the dictatorship of the butcher of the Shia and Kurds in Iraq, Saddam Hussein.

The civil war in Lebanon of the early 1970's that broke out as a result of the pressures exerted by the Palestinian refugees condemned to the ghettoes of exile in Lebanon as Sabra and Chatila in the oppressive social order of Lebanon through their military organizations as the Palestinian Liberation Organization (PLO) and the Popular Front for the Liberation of Palestine (PFLP). Both the PLO and the PLFP were secular organizations that disparaged Islamic discourse as the discourse to affect liberation and as such found themselves involved in an international futile order of military actions against civilians and alliances to elect such strikes.

Their international alliances with groups who found Islam anathema to their left wing adventurist post Marxist worldview meant in fact that the methodology for liberation was driven into the arms of those who would emerge as the proponents of the jihad against the greater kufr. In addition, this secular futile alliance would open the order of battle of the PLO, the PFLP and other groups to penetration and manipulation by covert agencies of western states as the US, Britain, France and the hand maiden of the west in the Middle East: Israel. In this cauldron of Lebanon the Shia would sit on the sidelines and watch as the Palestinians, the Sunni, the Christians and the Druze battle each other for hegemony over Lebanon in the early 1970's.

The Israeli invasion of Lebanon in the early 1970's led by Ariel Sharon bought and paid for by the west was a surgical strike to remove the PLO from Lebanon which was tacitly supported and tactically enabled by Syria's acquiescence. The genocide in the Palestinian ghettoes of Sabra and Chatila facilitated by the Christian militias and Syrian complicity sent telling messages of the military power of Israel, the impotence of the Arab world both militarily and morally and the birth of the Intifada.

Israel retreated from Beirut left it in the hands of the Syrians and created a security zone over southern Lebanon bordering Israel to be policed by their Christian militia allies. The Israeli invasion of Lebanon broke the back of the PLO and the PFLP as military organizations engaged with Israel. The PLO chose the wrong strategy, the wrong allies and wrong discourse with which to engage Israel with and for that mistake the Palestinians paid dearly, as is clearly seen in the futility of their actions in Gaza and the West Bank as Sabra and Chatila still exist, ghettoes of poverty, ignorance and underdevelopment.

The Israeli invasion of Lebanon and the subsequent occupation of Southern Lebanon would sow the seeds for the Shia awakening in Lebanon and the Sunni reaction to the Shia Intifada. The Iranian Islamic Revolution of 1979 would be the basis of Shia activism and military engagement in Lebanon and Iraq. The Shia of Lebanon chafing under the oppression of a caste system premised on religion and culture would rally on the call of the Islamic Revolution and Hezbollah built upon the theocratic structure in Shia Islam would engage the Israeli occupation of Southern Lebanon. It is Hezbollah that would carry out the military strikes against US forces in Lebanon particularly Beirut that would result in American military withdrawal from Lebanon.

Hezbollah's engagement with the Israeli and their Christian militia allies in southern Lebanon would enhance the hegemony of Syria over Beirut thereby ending the sectarian was between the Palestinian military organizations, the Christian militias, the Sunni Muslims and the Druze. For in the face of a resurgent Shia Intifada with an effective military arm Hezbollah, there was now need for peace and joint action in the face of the Shia challenge to the traditional caste system of Lebanon. The stage was now set for a common alliance between the west including the Soviet Union and the enemies of Shia Islam as Egypt, Syria, Jordan, Iraq and Saudi Arabia to engage militarily with Iran to roll back the Iranian Islamic Revolution.

The instrument was the butcher of Iraq, Saddam Hussein. His regime was then armed both conventionally and with weapons of mass destruction to wage war on the Iranian Islamic Revolution. In this war to roll back the Shia revolution the jihad against the greater kufr was born. Sunni Muslims and the organisations formed were trained, financed and deployed by the covert agencies of the west in their battle with Shia resurgence. Saudi Arabia played a major role in recruitment, training and financing of the jihad against the greater kufr. These Sunni Muslim organisations enjoyed then a close and functional relationship with the covert agencies of the west which explains their ability to travel to and from and create operational bases in the west.

The invasion of Afghanistan by the Soviet Union was in fact an attempt to incubate the Soviet empire from the virus of a resurgent Islam especially the virulent form Shia Islam. The quagmire of Afghanistan enabled the US and the Saudis to now include Pakistan into the alliance against the Soviet Empire and in so doing would make Pakistan its major operational base and the most potent incubator of the jihad against the greater kufr. It is in the Afghan refugee camps in Pakistan that the leadership of the Taliban would be drawn from and educated in the madrassas of Pakistan constituted by the discourse of the greater kufr. It is from the madrassas of Pakistan that the discourse of the greater kufr would wash over the Ummah of the world including Trinidad and Tobago. It is in Pakistan and Afghanistan that the covert agencies of the west and the Saudis created the critical mass that would explode upon the west with the fatwa of 1998.

It is then apparent that covert agencies, the ruling political elites of the west and Saudi Arabia fostered the creation of organisations but moreso a discourse of a specific jihad that would eventually lead to the attacks on targets in the west without ever grasping the potency, the operational acumen of this discourse in constituting military engagement with the west and Saudi Arabia. A danse macabre for limited pragmatic reasons was effected with individuals who would eventually turn on their benefactors because of the racist arrogance and blindness of the west to see the potential that this discourse of jihad possesses within the Ummah of the world.

In the literature on 9/11 conventional, mainstream and alternate discourse emerging out of North America especially the US there is an appalling lack of understanding on the nature and structure of the discourse against the greater kufr. There is the appalling failure to grasp that the Sunni Muslims who engaged and danced with the US did so to garner the order of battle of the west and the means to effect the military strikes in the west. And this is not the primary aim of their jihad against the greater kufr. For the primary aim is hegemony over the Arab Islamic world to the detriment of minorities dismissed as apostates: the Shia, the Kurds and Sufi Islam. Hegemony over the Arab Islamic world is simply the first step towards the launch of a bid for world conquest and the hegemony of Arab Islam under the rule of the Khalifa. For the Muslim who speaks Arabic is culturally Arab is the chosen race of their god destined to rule the world. A fatwa of Shaykh Ibn 'Uthayam states:

> "Marriage to such a Muslim who complies with the rulings of Islaam is permitted even though he does not know Arabic. There is a very strong case for him to marry a Muslim woman who is an Arab, in order that he might learn the Arabic language. There would be a lot of benefit for him in such a marriage.
> If then, this man is adhering to the rulings of Islaam, the marriage should go ahead, even though he does not speak Arabic. There is no objection to this happening.

This fatwa is but one instance of the racist hegemonist structure of the discourse of the jihad against the greater kufr. In this discourse Arab "Islam" stands purged of the moral imperatives of the Quran leaving in its place a discourse of racist hegemony bent upon world conquest which potently indicates the discursive antecedents of the discourse of the greater kufr is western discourse.

The endemic hate engendered by the discourse of the jihad against the greater kufr is indicated by two fatwas of Shakyh Ibn 'Uthaymeen as follows:

> "Question: Does not brotherhood extend to all of mankind because it is established that Aadam was the forefather of everyone?
> Response: This is not so. There is no doubt that everyone is from the offspring of Aadam but we don not say, 'This is my brother' when referring to a disbeliever meaning by that within the brotherhood of man. We can only refer to humans as brother when there is a relationship by descent or lineage."

> "There is no doubt that it is not permissible to call non-Muslims 'brothers'…
> Brotherhood, therefore is in faith. If, however, he were a brother by descent, it would be acceptable.
> This is acceptable when there is fraternal lineage. However, he is not your brother in religion. However, it is possible to find a way around this. He shouldn't say. 'Oh my brother' but rather he should say 'Oh brother' meaning by this, he is brother to whoever is his brother either in religion or through descent.
> In this way, he can attract him and soften his heart while not attributing brotherhood to himself. Hinting or allusion is a way out of lying."

There is then no singularity that is Allah's creation. This creation is fractured by a division between Muslim and non-believer. There is then no moral imperative that ensures the end of barbarity. The behavioural change that is the basis of the praxis of Allah (swt) revealed in the Quran is precluded for exclusion that forms the basis of a blood lust, a penchant for blood sacrifice and blood letting that generates a concept of god which is closer to the

Christian god of the Inquisition, the Crusades and European colonial domination than the praxis of Allah (swt).

In its quest for hegemony over the Arab Muslim world every moral imperative of the praxis of Allah (swt) is flouted, trampled on and clothed in a discourse of jihad against the greater kufr that renders them voiceless. The Ummah Wasat is then destined in the early years of the 21st century to experience the most potent threat to its existence and potency since European colonial domination. Not a single aspect of a Muslim's daily life would be spared the impact of the spawn of the west and it is the duty of Muslims in the west to wage jihad of the mouth, jihad at the level of the idea against this dajjal spawned by the west. The basis of this jihad at the level of the idea is the creation of a counter discourse, its articulation and dissemination to engage and disarm the discourse of the jihad against the greater kufr. This is my jihad, Inshallah.

In the October/November 1996 issue of Nida'ul Islam an interview with Osama Bin Laden was published. Bin Laden states:

> "What bears no doubt in this fierce Judaeo-Christian campaign against the Muslim world, the likes of which never has been seen before, is that the Muslims must prepare all the possible might to repel the enemy on the military, economic, missionary, and all other areas. It is crucial for us to be patient and to cooperate in righteousness and piety and to raise awareness to the fact that the highest priority, after faith is to repel the incursive enemy which corrupts the religion and the world, and nothing deserves a higher priority after faith, as the scholars have declared, for this cause, it is crucial to overlook many of the issues of bickering in order to unite our ranks so that we can repel the greater kufr."

The jihad against the greater kufr is defined as the military engagement with the Judaeo-Christian assault on Islam.

> "At the same time that some of the leaders are engaging in the major Kufr, which takes them out of the fold of Islam in broad daylight and in front of all the people, you will find a Fatwa from their religious organisation. In particular, the role of the religious organisation in the country of the two sacred mosques is of the most

ominous of roles, this is overlooking whether it fulfilled this role intentionally or unintentionally, the harm which eventuated from their efforts is no different from the role of the most ardent enemies of the nation."

Is there then a difference between the major kufr and the greater kufr?

"There were important efforts of the two explosions in Riyadh on both the internal and external aspects most important amongst these is the awareness of the people to the significance of the American occupation of the country of the two sacred mosques, and that the original decrees of the regime are a reflection of the wishes of the American occupiers. So the people became aware that their main problems were caused by the American occupiers and their puppets in the Saudi regime, whether this was from the religious aspect or from other aspects in their everyday lives."

The subservience of the house of Saud to the Judaeo-Christian crusaders, the mortal enemies of Islam constitute the greater kufr. The house of Saud pollutes the land of the two sacred mosques by first Islam and then by sacrificing the interests of Islam. The major and greater kufr then involves the nexus of the house of Saud, shirk and the American occupation of Saudi Arabia.

"These missions also paved the way for the raising of voices of opposition against the American occupation from within the ruling family and the armed forces."

This statement and the involvement of Bin Laden in the 1980's and the 1990's in the jihad against the communist regime of South Yemen reveals the dance of Sunni military organisations and individuals with US, Saudi Arabian and Pakistani covert agencies and powered elites.

In the April-May issue of Nida'ul Islam an article by Abu Abdul Aziz Al-Afghani in writing on the Islamic Taliban Movement states:

"The emergence of the Taliban Movement and its control over more than 80% of the Afghani lands has undoubtedly upset the equilibrium on the regional and international level. Thus, conspiracies were installed to influence it, in order to preserve the interests of various sides. These dangers that face the movement materialize as follows:

Firstly: The trials of assimilation.
Secondly: the Shiite-Communist Confederation."

For the Taliban Movement the Shia of Iran formed an alliance with the Soviet Union to subjugate Afghanistan to Iranian partition. The discourse of the Shia as shirk flows through the discourse of the Taliban Movement as it does with the discourse of the jihad against the greater kufr.

"Potentially the Movement may represent a strong force that will restore the dignity of Afghanistan's Jihadi movement so that it will resume the role of liberating the Islamic lands from the atheistic, faithless American tyranny. Particularly, after the mujahid Sheikh Usama bin Ladin declared war on the Crusade existence in the Arab region."

The Taliban Movement has also brought into the discourse of the jihad against the greater kufr recognizing the need to cleanse the Islamic lands of the crusaders and moreover Mujahid Sheikh Usama bin Ladin is the instrument of this jihad.

The signals, the warnings were being published in 1996, 1997 long before the first attack on the New York World Trade Center and the attack of 2001 on the same Manhattan, New York landmark. The 2001 attack was not as a result of a massive failure of intelligence, or as a result of the complicity of the covert agencies and the powered elites with bin Laden or as a result of a covert operation of the Mossad. The powered elites of the west especially the US must accept that it was a phenomenal failure of perception. It was a catastrophic failure of a racist Orientalist discourse to see the potency of Islamic discourse, to see that an alliance was formed to wage war on the Shia and Communist atheist with Sunni militarists who utilized this alliance to gather and garner the access, the material, the finances and the organizational acumen to launch attacks at their primary enemy: the nexus of the House of Saud and the US.

To date all of the explanations and exposes of the realities of September 2001 and subsequent attacks fail to articulate on the part of the west a knowledge of, a respect for Islamic discourse in all its complexities. Alas the west is unable to do so, it is in fact precluded from doing so by dint of the racist Orientalist discourse through which it sees, constitutes Muslims. The military engagement with Islam that exploded in brutal intensity in 1983 with the truck bombings by shahids of US and French forces in Beirut, Lebanon has now exploded into a worldwide engagement, a battle royal for hegemony.

Long before the spawn of the west moved to military engagement with the west in their cities, we the Muslims of the Ummah Wasat have paid with our lives for denouncing the spawn of the west, the dajjal of the 21st century. In those days the spawn of the west was the plaything of the west, their hitmen and heavies in their battles with the Shia and the Marxist regimes of the Cold War. We seek no alliance with the incubator of the dajjal in our jihad of the mouth to silence this discourse of jihad within the Ummah Wasat. For the price to be paid for a dance macabre with the west is the very sustainability of the Ummah Wasat. Today we are in the midst of the greatest most potent threat to the Ummah Wasat since the hijra. And we are all called to arms by the praxis of Allah (swt). To this end I devote my life Inshallah.

THE DIVERSITY OF ISLAMIC DISCOURSE

A shabnama/political pamphlet that appeared on the 1st November 1995 dealing with the Taliban and what distinguishes it discursively from the other Islamic groups in Afghanistan presents a potent example of the diversity that is Islamic Discourse. What is noteworthy is that the said pamphlet appeared in Washington DC. USA. The pamphlet states:

> "The concept of the organization of the Taliban is primordial to all other Islamic movements and organizations throughout the Islamic world such as the Ikhwan-ul-Muslimeen and that of Wahabism."

The position is that the Taliban as an organic structure of Islam in Afghanistan pre-dates all other organisations that are involved in Afghanistan of the 1990's.

> "The organization of the Taliban and the Mullahs has historically proven to be the front line defender of the national integrity and the religion of Islam. Contemporary Afghan history is littered with records of the vital roles, which the forces of the Taliban and the

Mullahs have played as front line soldiers in all major wars in Afghan history.

The Taliban and Mullahs have always been the vanguard of jihad in Afghanistan in the wars with the kafir. It is then expected in 2004 that the Taliban and Mullahs would continue the war in Afghanistan against the kufr.

"When the Taliban, soon after the so-called Communist Saur Revolution, proclaimed the jihad and were in the process of its practical implementation, they had no knowledge of the association of some other Afghan Muslim groups and organizations led by Gulbudin Hekmatyar, Burhanudin Rabaini and Ahmad Shah Masood with Zulfikar Ali Bhutto and the Jama'at Islami of Pakistan. These individuals had been trained at the Balaherar of Peshawar by Pakistanis like Nasrullah Babar. They were not trained for the defending of the Afghan national integrity but as Pakistani political tools to be used against the then Afghan President, Sardar Daud Khan. Similarly, when the Taliban were in their initial stages of fighting the Russian forces, they had neither heard of General Zia Ul Haq, nor of Hassan-ul-bana and Sayed Qutb, the latter a theoretician of the Muslim brotherhood, nor any of the Wahabi Group. These Islamic groups were all deemed by the Afghan Taliban as part of 'Jama'ats" or "organizational" elements who had deviated from the right path."

The Taliban and Mullahs have therefore refused to be polluted by consorting with Pakistani agencies but they have pronounced the fatwa of shirk upon Jama'ati Islami of Mawdudi, Ikhwan al Muslimun of Sayed Qutb and the Wahhabiyya of Saudi Arabia.

"The Taliban neither knew of the idea of revolution nor do they believe in it today. The Taliban have never recognized anything over and beyond a strict adherence to the Book of Allah, Holy Quran, and the Sonat, or the deeds and teachings of Prophet Muhammad (PBUH)."

The Taliban reject the concept of the Islamic Revolution renouncing the concept as being outside the pale of Islam.

> "It was due to the initial sacrifices and the opening up of travel routes by the religious class and the Afghan public that enabled the so-called 'organized' Mujahideen groups, trained in Pakistan, to bring in their Arab 'friends' and, hence act as 'heroes' in the Afghan Jihad films made by the BBC and various other western media sources."

Does this specific discourse of the Taliban view Osama Bin Laden as one of their Arab friends?

> "There is no doubt that General Zia believed in the promotion of Islamic fundamentalism. He was a firm believer in the myth of an Islamic revolution carried out by the fundamentalist movements throughout the Islamic world. This is against the beliefs of the Taliban. The Taliban do not advocate the idea of a global Muslim revolution in collaboration with the Ikhwani forces who are seen to have deviated from the path of the Shariat and the teachings of the Quran and that of the Prophet Muhammad (PBUH)."

The Ikhwani and Wahhabis fighters in Afghanistan were brought into the jihad against the Soviet Union to serve the interests of Pakistan. The shirk imported set about the creation of a geo-political crisis that resulted in the removal of the Taliban from power by the west following the events of 11th September 2001 which has regenerated the need for jihad against the kufr in Afghanistan once again.

> "The current Taliban movement is, however, an integrative movement, having in its ranks different Taliban from various regions as well as former army officers.
> 1.   The Local Taliban
> This group of the Taliban follows the teachings of Islam based on the Sonat, or the deeds and teachings of Mohammed (PBUH), and advocates the idea of the Shariat based on the principles of 'Adela and Arbe'a' or Four Imams, a school of thought which is in the

> sub-continent referred to as the Daiwband School of thought. In a way, they are the 'real mc coy' and are the most resistant to the influences of western civilization and the beliefs and values associated with it. Bound by social and material adversity, the group of the local Taliban avoids the life of the 'shine and gold'. This group, nevertheless, has constituted the very pivot of Taliban movement, both during the jihad against the Soviet forces and in the current Taliban movement. To associate these 'momens', or righteous Taliban, to foreign forces and centres of influence is nothing short of a great sin."

The local Taliban is then the core of the Taliban and the nucleus of the Taliban resurgence against the kufir occupation of Afghanistan at present, but this Taliban adheres to the jurisprudence of the Hanafis and the specific discourse of the Deoband school of thought with its focus on the Prophet Muhammad (uwbp).

> "From very early days, the Taliban, based on their adherence to the Sunni school of thought, were steadfastly opposed to the presence of the Salafyoon, whether in the guise of the Wahabis or Ikhwaris. Even in their Jihadi ranks, the Taliban would not give such elements a chance to come to the fore. As a result the specific Islamic predilections of the Salafyoon in the pre-communist society remained confined to the precincts of the education and Government institutions. The general understanding among the religious scholars was that these elements were in actual reality the product of the government's policies."

The Salafyoon, those of Salafiyya are those who have polluted Islamic praxis therefore they are shirk. Osama Bin Laden and Al Qaeda in keeping with this discourse of the Taliban are of the Salafyoon, the denizens of salafiyya.

> "Today, these fundamentalist groups have left such a legacy of foreign interference behind that no patriotic movement, including the Taliban, can avoid its effects. Foreign interference, today, intermingled with geopolitical imperatives, presents itself in such an ubiquitous form that its role is not only unavoidable but undeniable. The

simple-minded and inexperienced Taliban are today unable to deal adequately with the existence of such imperatives and the extent of the deep-rooted foreign interference."

"The Taliban too have proven to be vulnerable to foreign interference."

The legacy of the salafyoon and the mistakes and failings of Taliban leadership culminated in the overthrow of the Taliban regime in Afghanistan by the military intervention of the west. The discourse of the organic Taliban offers understanding of two Afghan realities since the invasion of the west post September 11th, 2001. These are: (a) the abiding failure to crush the Taliban and capture leading figures of its elite that wielded state power. (b) The ease with which foreign fighters were given up to the invading forces of the west.

In an interview with Ma'soum Afghani Taliban ambassador to Pakistan published by Nida'ul Islam, April-May Issue 1997, Afghani states when questioned on the relationship of the Taliban with the Arab Mujahideen as follows:

> "This relationship is based on this: the Arabs fulfilled their role in Jihad and Afghanistan against communism. We have relationships with some of them but not all of them are under our control or on our land. They live in Afghanistan as guests, but the land of Afghanistan will not be used against any other Islamic country."

Clearly the role of the Arab mujahideen in Afghanistan is now over with the defeat of communism. There is no role for them in governance and they are in fact a potential threat to the peace and stability of Afghanistan. Osama Bin Laden had then to be of specific strategic importance to the Taliban ruling elite to be granted presence and occupational mobility and effectiveness in Afghanistan. The Taliban regime paid for its failure to abide by the very discourse articulated in the pamphlet studied.

CONCLUSION

The documents presented in this study of the discourse of Al Qaeda were reviewed and chosen for deconstruction not simply because they were attributed to Al Qaeda by the media which published them. One can posit that given the covert war of the west against proponents of jihad, documents attributed to Al Qaeda can then be manufactured. To create such documents the composers must then be fluent in the streams of Islamic discourse and knowledgeable to situate the document within a stream, which flows with the corpus of jihadi discourse made public outside of the west especially in this age of globalized telecommunications.

The initial action is then a deconstruction to question the bona fide of the document. Specific discursive concepts, structures and signposts are sought. Expressions that indicate that the writer is in fact a practising Muslim are perhaps the most potent indicators sought for it is very easy for a Muslim like myself to pick up a secular atheist purporting to construct a document that flows in Islamic discourse. Such knowledge we must not reveal for we must preserve the ability to unearth the terminators sent amongst the Ummah Wasat passing themselves off as Muslims.

To this end I am not obliged to point out, to name the documents contained in my anthology attributed to Al Qaeda and others that viewed with suspicion on my part. For it is necessary to present all discourse of whatever species, of whatever party as this illustrates that it is a struggle first at the level of the idea, framed and articulated via discourse. The primary task of the Muslim is then to formulate and articulate a discourse of liberation grounded, founded, rooted only in the Praxis of Allah (swt) as is only revealed in the Holy Quran.

STATEMENT OF INTENT

What follows is a presentation of selections from the Holy Qur'an and the Hadith of the Prophet Muhammad (uwbp). By no stretch of the imagination am I embarking on a journey of exegesis of the text of the Holy Qur'an and the Hadith of the Prophet (uwbp). What follow is simply selections of the Holy Qur'an, the text revealed (wahy) and recorded that speak to humans across linear time.

The selections are based upon specific issues addressed by the revelation so recorded in the Qur'an, the discourse constituted as a result and its relevance to specific issues in the daily lives of Muslims in Trinidad.

It is therefore an attempt to provide for the non-Muslim reader of my text a crude route map to enable them during this journey through Islamic discourse to "see", to perceive the way in which the Islamic worldview constitutes the world.

The Holy Qur'an brought into existence by revelation (wahy) can then only be and is the foundation of Islamic discourse. Wahy is the action and decision of Allah thereby it is part of the praxis of Allah. The Hadith is the textual expressions, recordings of the discourse and praxis of the Prophet Muhammad (uwbp), which was the outcome of his specific relationship with the praxis of Allah expressed via the Prophethood of Muhammad (uwbp).

The discursive praxis of the Prophet (uwbp) is then the ultimate praxis of submission to the will of Allah, the praxis of Allah, in this age of wahy that culminates in the Day of Judgment. The Holy Qur'an and the Hadith taken together affords the Muslim the following:

(a) The praxis of Allah which reveals the nature of Allah and the path/praxis that enables humankind to realize their fullest potential as the creation of Allah.
(b) The praxis of the Prophet Muhammad (uwbp) which is the praxis of submission to the will of Allah, of Islam.

The praxis of the Prophet Muhammad (uwbp) reaches across history, linear time, in its relentless relevance to the Muslim seeking guidance on the path of Islam in his/her daily life.

Repeated journeys through the texts of the Holy Qur'an and the Hadith of the Prophet Muhammad (uwbp) have indicated to me the irreversible contradictions that exist between Western discourse and Islam.

The praxis of Allah insists most unapologetically that Allah is the only totality that exists full stop, per se, without limitations. And as such no rational, positivist, empiricist methodology can discern, can attest to the totality of Allah. There is simply no methodology forged outside the bounds of wahy that can deduce, attest to, and confirm the existence of Allah.

The concept of the secular totality conceived on the epistemology of secular positivist science, which was purportedly so potent in battering down the doors of theologies everywhere, is simply then anathema to Islamic discourse.

These twain shall never meet and whenever social engineers who are really social alchemist's attempt to blend both discourses the explosion in the laboratory is self-evident, manifest (Inshallah). The inherent duality of the white man's Western discourse, which is a by-product of their relentless striving to deny the potency of death, and the consequential relentless striving to constitute streams of "Others" finds only irreconcilable contradiction with Islamic discourse.

The only duality is Allah for out of Allah flows life and death, realization and separation.

The Day of Judgment insists that the duality is Allah for all must stand in judgment, both believer and unbeliever.

In effect the only "Other" in the praxis of Allah is humankind for Allah is the supreme subject, the creator of a specific discourse for humankind that constitutes praxis for transcending the finality of death. Wahy is then an intrusion, a discursive break, and a discursive rupture in the flow of Jahiliyya or the discourse of ignorance. Revelation then deliberately, purposively breaks, ruptures the discursive flow of human endeavour in the realm of Jahiliyya. Allah can only do this for Allah is the only totality, duality in supreme and sublime existence.

Wahy then presents a discursive order, a discursive structure and flow, which must always be in contradiction with any discursive structure, which refuses to recognize and accept the central tenets of WAHY. Herein lies the central core, the nucleus of this irreconcilable contradiction between Islam and the white man's discourse.

The discursive flow from Western Christianity to secular positivist scientism was possible through the centrality of the individual, human reason and death in the discursive structures of the white man. In fact the core of the white man's discursive structure is the danse macabre of the white man and death perceived through human reason.

Whereas in Islamic discourse the core of the discourse is Allah revealed in the praxis of Allah. The praxis of Allah revealed to humankind in the Holy Qur'an relentlessly beckons to humankind insisting that the only path to transcend death is the praxis of submission to Allah's will.

Human reason is secondary in fact peripheral to the whole process for human reason not founded upon wahy is flawed and unable to give humankind the means to attain the Praxis of Allah. The Praxis of Allah therefore insists that the Muslim must deconstruct the discourse of Jahiliyya and replace it with the discourse of Islam and its attendant praxis towards attainment of the state of transcendence of all that it is to be human, finite and flawed.

The Muslim addresses his/her individual, specifically personal path through a praxis of submission to Allah's will applicable to every instance of existence as a Muslim. But the praxis of Allah relentlessly calls, beckons to the Muslim to refuse the individualization of his/her submission to the will of Allah.

For the praxis calls for, constitutes a community of believers and the praxis of the community or Ummah.

In Islamic discourse there is then no individual who is a juridical subject empowered with rights under law. Neither is there the central individual empowered through descent by a bloodline that at some time in it's dim past mingled with God.

Both Monarchy and Western democracy and all they constitute are anathema to Islamic discourse for they are founded on concepts of the individual that are incongruent with the Praxis of Allah.

Finally to the readers of my text I ask that the discourse of the Praxis of Allah (SWT), which would be sampled, be allowed to resonate in your perceptive structures throughout your journey through this text.

For this is the only way to link the praxis of a Muslim and the discourse that constitutes that praxis enabling the viewer to appreciate the reality that Islam is an alternate worldview, an alternate praxis with its alternate discursive structures.

And the only way to understand this reality is to accept the validity of its existence and the structures of human perception constituted by Islamic discourse.

Western academia can only remove the Orientalist/racist scales from its eyes when it accepts that there are valid alternate worldviews which reject all that constitutes its worldview.

SELECTIONS FROM THE HOLY QUR'AN

Translated by M.H. Shakir (1993 N.Y.)

SURAH 1; THE OPENING

(1) In the Name of Allah, the Beneficent, the Merciful.

(2) All praise is due to Allah, the Lord of the Worlds.

(3) The Beneficent, the Merciful.

(4) Master of the Day of Judgment.

(5) Thee do we serve and Thee do we beseech for help.

(6) Keep us on the right path.

(7) The path of those upon whom Thou has bestowed favors. Not (the path) of those upon whom Thy wrath is brought down, nor of those who go astray.

SURAH 59; THE BANISHMENT

(22) He is Allah besides whom there is no God, the Knower of the unseen and seen; He is the Beneficent, the Merciful.

(23) He is Allah, besides whom there is no God; the King, the Holy, the Giver of Peace, the Granter of Security, Guardian over all, the Mighty, the Supreme, the Possessor of every greatness; Glory be to Allah from what they set up (with him).

(24) He is Allah, the Creator, the Maker, the Fashioner; His are the most excellent names; whatever is in the heavens and the earth declares His Glory; and He is the Mighty, the Wise.

Sura 1 or the Fatiah and verses 22-24 of Sura 59 are presented as a selection of the ample instances in the Holy Qur'an of the centrality of Allah in Islamic discourse, and by extension the ortho-praxis of Islam.

SURA 2; THE COW

(256) There is no compulsion in religion; truly the right way has become clearly distinct from error; therefore, whoever disbelieves in the Shaitan and believes in Allah, he indeed has laid hold on the firmest handle, which shall not break off, and Allah is Hearing, Knowing.

SURA 3; THE FAMILY OF IMRAN

(110) You are the best of the nations raised up for (the benefit of man); you enjoin what is right and forbid the wrong and believe in Allah;

SURA 13; THE THUNDER

(11).... surely Allah does not change the condition of a people until they change their own condition, and when Allah intends evil to a people, there is no averting it, and besides Him they have no protector.

The three selections quoted above together form the basis of Islamic discourse of especial relevance to Muslim minorities in the West. Three salient points of the verses quoted are all linked with the praxis of Islamic discourse.

Firstly there is no compulsion in religion; hence the entry into the spaces of Islamic discourse must be predicated on action driven by free will.

Therefore the propagation of Islamic discourse (da'wa) is incumbent upon the Ummah, based on the free will, choice of individuals to both propagate and submit to the Praxis of Allah (SWT).

Secondly, for the Ummah, the community of believers, Muslims it is incumbent upon them to apply the potent watchwords, which are in fact the basis of ortho-praxis of Islamic discourse.

To enjoin what is good and forbid what is evil is a stipulation of Allah (swat) placed upon every believer, every member of the community of Allah.

The criterion that defines good from evil is not based on human reason but on the wahy of Allah (SWT), contained in the Holy Qur'an.

Good and evil as defined by Allah (SWT) through wahy is then constant, timeless and cannot be revoked save and except by the promulgator of such criterion, Allah (SWT).

Thirdly just as humankind has the free choice of will to accept or reject the praxis of Allah, humankind especially the Ummah is called to self-reliant action towards attaining goals set.

The praxis of Allah is never fatalistic for the believer, the Ummah are relentlessly charged with a praxis of action.

SURAH 2 THE ALLIES
(21) Certainly you have in the Apostle of Allah an excellent exemplar for him who hopes in Allah and the latter day and remembers Allah much.

SURAH 7; THE ELEVATED PLACES
(158) Say; O people! Surely I am the Apostle of Allah to you all, of Him Whose is the Kingdom of the heavens and the earth, there is no God but He; He brings to life and causes to die, therefore believe in Allah and His apostle, the Ummi Prophet who believes in Allah and his words, and follow him so that you may walk in the right way.

The Ummi Prophet Muhammad (uwbp) the excellent exemplar to all Muslims has in his praxis of submission to the will of Allah left a legacy of insight and practices that constitute then the praxis of the Prophet Muhammad as recorded in the Hadith.

SURA 22; THE PILGRIMAGE.

(39) Permission (to fight) is given to those upon whom war is made because they are oppressed, and most surely Allah is well able to assist them, (40) Those who have been expelled from their homes without a just cause except that they say; Our Lord is Allah. And had there not been Allah's repelling some people by others, certainly there would have been pulled down cloisters and churches and synagogues and mosques in which Allah's name is much remembered; and surely Allah will help him who helps His cause; most surely Allah is Strong, Mighty.

SURAH 9; REPENTANCE

(20) Those who believed and fled (their homes) and strove hard in Allah's way with their property and their souls are much higher in rank with Allah; and those are they who are the achievers (of their objects).

(111) Surely Allah has bought of the believers their persons and their property for this, that they shall have the garden; they fight in Allah's way, so they slay and are slain; a promise which is binding on him in the Taurat and the Injeel and the Qur'an; and who is more faithful to his covenant than Allah? Rejoice therefore in the pledge, which you have made; and that is the mighty achievement.

The praxis of enjoining good and forbidding evil requires of the Ummah at specific instances in its relations with unbelievers/Jahiliyya the waging of war. To oppress the Ummah for its praxis of Allah, to attempt to destroy the houses of worship of Allah are noteworthy flash points or conjunctures that place jihad on the agenda of the praxis of Islam.

It is then up to the Ummah to decide upon what courses of action it would adopt within the praxis of Islam.

SURAH 109; THE UNBELIEVERS.

In the name of Allah, the Beneficent, the Merciful.

(1) Say; O Unbelievers!

(2) I do not serve that, which you serve,

(3) Nor do you serve Him whom I serve,

(4) Nor am I going to serve that which you serve,

(5) Nor are you going to serve Him whom I serve,

(6) You shall have your religion and I shall have my religion.

SURAH 112; THE UNITY

In the name of Allah, the Beneficent, the Merciful

(1) Say; He, Allah is One,

(2) Allah is He on whom all depend.

(3) He begets not, nor is he begotten.

(4) And none is like him.

Surah's 112 and 109 are perhaps fitting to end the selections from the Holy Qur'an with. For Surah 112 affirms the Tawhid of Allah, the unity of singularity in existence, and the basis for the perceptual gulf that separates Islam from the West.

Whilst Surah 109 succinctly expresses the geography of the spaces in which the praxis/the discourse of Allah reigns supreme, juxtaposed in its specificities of existence to the spaces in which Jahiliyya reigns supreme. And in the words of Surah 109 the twain shall never meet, for to even envisage such a meeting, a syncretism is abomination, shirk.

Surah 109 envisages peaceful co-existence but Jahiliyya can never be allowed to conquer, to taint the spaces under the hegemony of the praxis of Allah.

SELECTIONS FROM THE HADITH OF THE PROPHET MUHAMMAD (uwbp) The praxis of the Prophet Muhammad (uwbp) that transcended racism as directed by the Holy Qur'an/the praxis of Allah.

The Hadith is reported by al-Bukhari, Muslim and Abu Dawood. It states:

> "One day a heated discussion arose between Abu Dharr and a black man named Bilal who was a former slave of Abyssinian origin. Abu Dharr, in anger derogatively called him a black woman's son. The Prophet (uwbp) was highly irritated by the insulting remark and said to Abu Dharr," How dare you abuse him by his mother's color? Traces of the times of ignorance (Jahiliyya) still remain within you!"

The Prophet (uwbp) went on to say:

"You have overstepped the bounds (of Islam). A white woman's son is not in any way superior to a black woman's son except due to greater piety and righteousness." Upon hearing this, Abu Dharr, in shame, put his face in the ground and begged Bilal to step over it."

Hadith as recorded by Muslim states:

"Ayesha (may Allah be pleased with her) states; "The Holy Prophet (uwbp) never beat anyone-neither a woman nor a servant-although he fought in the cause of Allah. If he was ever harmed by anyone, he would not avenge himself. But whenever a sacred place of Allah was desecrated, he would take revenge for the sake of Allah."

This Hadith indicates the praxis of the Prophet (uwbp) in regards to the cause of war in the name of Allah, a potent relevant praxis to be emulated by all Muslims through time.

Hadith as recorded by Abu Daoud states:

"On the authority of Abu Saeed (may Allah be pleased with him), who said; The Messenger of Allah (uwbp) said; "The best jihad is when a person speaks the truth before a tyrant ruler"."

Both Hadith then enumerate the basis of the praxis of Jihad of the Prophet (uwbp). The praxis teaches that the primary strategy is engagement with the enemies of Allah for the sake of the Praxis of Allah. Jihad is then multi faceted from enjoining good and forbidding evil by public testimony of the Muslim to engagement in military actions.

Hadith as recorded by Muslim states:

"On the authority of Abu Saeed Al-Khudri (may Allah be pleased with him), who said; The Messenger of Allah (uwbp) said; "Anybody amongst you who notices something evil should correct it with his own hands. If he is unable to do so, he should correct it with his tongue. If he is unable to do this, he should at least consider it as bad in his heart; for this is the lowest degree of faith."

The praxis of the Prophet (uwbp) on the issue of interpersonal relations within the Ummah. Hadith as recorded by Muslim states:

> "On the authority of Abu Hurairah (may Allah be pleased with him), who said; "The Messenger of Allah uwbp) said; "Do not envy another; do not inflate prices one to another; do not hate one another; do not turn away from one another; and do not undercut one another, but be you, O servants of Allah, brothers. A Muslim is the brother of a Muslim; he neither oppresses him nor does he fail him, he neither lies to him nor does he hold him in contempt. Piety is right here (and he pointed to his breast three times). It is evil enough for a man to hold his brother Muslim in contempt. It is absolutely a sin for a Muslim to kill another, or to take his property or to destroy his honor."

A Hadith of singular importance to the study of the relations between the Muslims of the Ummah of Trinidad leading up to the military action of July 27th 1990 by the Jamaat al Muslimeen.

Finally in closing this section of Hadith and the text dealing with the Holy Qur'an and the Hadith of the Prophet Muhammad (uwbp). Hadith recorded by Muslim states:

> "On the authority of Abu Hurairah (may Allah be pleased with him) who said; "The Messenger of Allah uwbp) said; "The world is prison for the believer, and Paradise for the disbeliever"."

THE FUTURE AGENDA

The salient reality of this text is the pressing need for Islamic jurisprudence that focuses on Muslim minorities in the west. There must then be developed a jurisprudence for the praxis of an Islamic minority in the capitalist social order of the west. The primary focus of this Islamic minority has to be da'wah and all other considerations must be subservient to the overriding strategy for sustainable da'wah towards the propagation of the din in the west.

To realise a sustainable strategy of da'wah Islamic discourse and jurisprudence grounded in the Quran is the prime necessity. To this end the basis of Islamic jurisprudence that presently exists has to be questioned critically.

"Read your book, your own self is sufficient as a reckoner against you this day."

(Surah The Israelites: 14)

"...for only the delivery of the message is (incumbent) on you, while calling (them) to account is our (business).

(Surah The Thunder: 40)

To read the Quran and da'wah are then imperatives of Islam. Every Muslim is then obligated to study the Quran and to propagate the din. A sustainable da'wah in a post-modern western capitalist social order can only be realised via the articulation of Islamic discourse grounded in the Quran that addresses the unique and specific realities of daily life in the west and moreso the discourse of post-modern western capitalism.

A search of the Quran to uncover the revelation that transcends time of relevance to the post-modern era of the west is the starting point for the journey towards articulation of Islamic discourse that addresses western sensibilities. The crisis of the Ummah in the early 21st century is multifaceted but the cusp of the crisis is the articulation of streams of purported Islamic discourse that refuse, cannot see the realities of the west much less articulate a discourse that the west can hear. Purported Islamic discourse in denial is the result of a jurisprudence that has relentlessly attempted to shackle, to limit revelation that transcends time to a praxis that is unchanging, purportedly sacred, sacrosanct and immutable.

These discourses of shirk posing as Islamic discourse have attempted to muzzle revelation for fear of its power to destroy and deconstruct man made tradition that is passed off as immutable. The crisis of this shirk is that Muslims of these persuasions are willing and have relentlessly slaughtered Muslims over time to maintain the hegemony of this shirk. Revelation made to the Prophet (pbuh) that transcends time can never be limited by a praxis that is manmade neither can manmade praxis transcend time.

It is only with the march of time and the appearance of specific epistemes in the history of man would the revelation relevant to this specific episteme be perceptible to the Muslims of that specific episteme. This is so because knowledge is never cumulative and the only knowledge that transcends time is Allah's (swt) revelation, which is never and can never be cumulative. In Islam there is no Son of God, there is no intermediary between God and man. There is only revelation, the Quran that stretches in expanse from its initial revelation to the end of time. No human can perceive and hold within the limits of a finite mind the expanse, time transcendence that is Allah (swt) as revealed in the Quran.

All that is constant in Islam is then revelation, the Quran. The movement to create jurisprudence that is transcendent was and is then shirk. The rule of thumb is then that whenever in an episteme the jurisprudence stands as a hindrance, a barrier to sustainable da'wah then the jurisprudence has to be at fault and has to be re-formulated. Such is the reality of the early 21st century in the west and the purported streams of Islamic discourse that have effectively hindered if not destroyed sustainable da'wah in the west.

The present streams of Islamic jurisprudence are the hybrid products of the blending of non-Quranic discourse with the Quran to formulate schools of jurisprudence. This was the initial mistake made, the flaw, the aberration that resulted in the vain attempt to shackle revelation to jurisprudence. This aberration hardened when the western discourse of truth positivist science was added to the brew. Muslims seduced by the west willingly surrendered to the western discourse of science and scientific methodology in an attempt to 'modernise' Islam.

One example of this seduction is the concept of the Islamization of knowledge project, a misnomer in terms. To Islamise western knowledge is in effect to state that the backwardness of the Ummah is as a direct result of hindrances in the worldview of the Ummah and the means to end this is to Islamise a knowledge base that is anathema to the Quran. Likewise they speak of Quranic sciences, which is another misnomer in terms and an indication of the inferiority that plagues non-white ex-colonial races of the world.

The Quran is revelation and there is no need to speak of a Quranic science for the Quran is one Quran with all its terms of references for itself and in itself. The Quran affirms itself and confirms itself therefore there is Islamic discourse so charged with these tasks and Quranic methodology that drives the discourse. It is the sole duty of every Muslim to discover and become fully versed in Quranic methodology and the discourse that is produced and contained within the ambit of the revelation. Da'wah is then the articulation of Islamic discourse that is relevant to the episteme in which the Muslim is positioned in time. The Quran affirms its relevance across time, the transcendence of time that is the preserve of revelation; therefore any failure of Islamic discourse to be relevant to any episteme is the fault of the Ummah.

> "And with the truth have We revealed it, and with truth did it come; and We have not sent you but as the giver of good news and as a warner."

> (Surah The Israelites: 105)

> "Whatsoever communications we abrogate or cause to be forgotten, we bring one better than it or like it. Do you not know that Allah has power over all things?"

> (Surah The Cow: 106)

THE CASE OF THE EXECUTION OF THE APOSTATE

Can a Muslim minority in the west insist that the execution of apostates/backsliders from Islam is in fact Islamic praxis? In the episteme of the post-modern western capitalist order can a Muslim minority of the west maintain its integrity and execute sustainable da'wah by executing an apostate? The Quran states:

> "Surely (as for) those who return on their backs after that guidance has become manifest to them, the Shaitan has made it a light matter to them; and he gives them respite. That is because they say to those who hate what Allah has revealed: We will obey you in some of the affairs; and Allah knows their secrets.
> But how will it be when the angels cause them to die smiting their backs?"

> (Sura Muhammad: 25,26,27)

> "Surely those who disbelieve and turn away from Allah's way and oppose the Apostle after that guidance has become clear to them (cannot) harm Allah in any way, and He will make null their deeds."

> (Sura Muhammad: 32)

"Surely those who disbelieve and turn away from Allah's way, then they die while they are unbelievers, Allah will by no means forgive them."

(Sura Muhammad: 34)

The Quran states:

"What is the matter with you, then, you have become two parties about the hypocrites, while Allah has made them return (to unbelief) for what they have earned? Do you wish to guide him whom Allah has caused to err? And whomsoever Allah causes to err, you shall by no means find a way to him. They desire that you should disbelieve as they have disbelieved, so that you might be (all) alike; therefore take not from among friends until they fly (their homes) in Allah's way; but if they turn back, then seize them and kill them wherever you find them, and take not from among them a friend or a helper.
…therefore if they withdraw from you and do not fight you and offer you peace, then Allah has not given you a way against them.
You will find others who desire that they should be safe from you and secure from their own people; as often as they are sent back to the mischief they get thrown into it headlong; therefore if they do not withdraw from you, and (do not) offer you peace and restrain their hands, then seize them and kill them wherever you find them; and against these we have given you a clear authority."

(Sura Women: 88-90)

The execution of the hypocrites is an action triggered by the hostile aggression of the hypocrites to the Ummah. It is then a defensive war by the Ummah against the acts of aggression of the hypocrites/munafikun.

Whenever the hypocrites call for peace the defensive war of the Ummah has to end. In the face of non-aggression by the hypocrites to the Ummah there is no need for a defensive war, and a war of conquest by the Ummah against the hypocrites is not authorised by the Quran. For hypocrisy, apostasy/backsliding is the will of Allah (swt) and the Ummah simply does not have the wherewithal to change this state of separation from, this condemnation from Allah (swt). It is only Allah (swt) who can reverse this condition of existence.

There is then no Quranic basis for the execution of apostates in states dominated by Muslims and in Islamic states. In any geographical entity where Muslims dominate, apostates within this entity can in no way mount a war of aggression to trigger the defensive war of the Ummah. Moreso capital punishment for apostasy within Islamic states or in the states where Muslims are the dominant majority is not permitted by the Quran.

Muslim minorities of the west can in no way at present launch a defensive war against the aggression of the apostates/backsliders and the hypocrites. We simply do not constitute an independent entity, a state with the revenues, laws and personnel to execute a defensive war. We are then precluded to utilise the resources at hand to ensure that the Ummah co-exists peacefully with the apostates/backsliders and hypocrites.

The Ummah is called upon to engage with the political system, the judicial system to ensure that every single right endowed upon us as citizens of the west are in fact respected as we exercise them. Rather than seeking to become invisible the Ummah has to be locally and nationally visible which demands that the worldview that seeks to replicate a jurisprudence that is irrelevant and injurious to da'wah in the west has to be purged. Faced with aggression in the west the Ummah must be willing to respond with non-violent resistance to the point where we flee the persecution as refugees from anti-Muslim aggression for this is the only strategy that preserves the potency of da'wah in the west.

Military engagement in the west by the Ummah is a pipe dream, a dangerous worldview that facilitates nihilist adventurism as the attacks on New York and Madrid. These attacks have done nothing for the advancement of da'wah in the west or to expose the rapacious imperialism of specific powered elites of the west. Those of us of the Ummah of the west who were born, raised, socialised and educated in the west embraced Islam for what Islam inherently is i.e. the discourse of TAWHID. We are then charged with the task of articulating Islamic discourse as contained in the Quran for this episteme of postmodern western capitalism. We are then charged with da'wah to this episteme and the formulation of Islamic jurisprudence for this episteme. To fail in these tasks is to invite the wrath of Allah (swt).

The Ummah Wasat of the west today faces not only the threat of a virulent anti-Islam crusade but by far its most potent adversary is within the Ummah

Wasat. The discourse of purdah, Arab racist hegemony, and a backward ideational cocoon that is attempting to strangle the revelation that is the Quran with backwardness. This ideational backwardness has surrendered to the west at the level of the idea and is premised upon Muslim self-immolation hence its penchant for futile extremism and adventurism.

The Al Qaeda discourse of the greater kufr is today the most potent example of Muslim self-immolation as the basis for extremism and futile military adventurism for it is premised on ideational backwardness with all its oppressive manifestations: male hegemony, Arab hegemony, discursive hegemony and internecine warfare. The potent threat that instances of these allegedly Islamic discourses pose to sustainable da'wah in the west is the refusal of these discourses to give primacy to the revelation, the Quran.

These alleged Islamic discourses seek to replicate in the west structures and worldviews which are not sustainable in the west and by so doing declare the west to be hostile to Islam and an infertile expanse of civilization impervious to da'wah thereby justifying extremism and military adventurism. By extension this allegedly Islamic position also invalidates the revelations of the Quran for persons who call themselves Muslims are in fact insisting that an episteme can arise that is impervious to the call of Allah (swt) to the creation of Allah (swt) for redemption, for liberation.

This is a praxis of shirk that demands that all Muslims who live in submission to Allah (swt) wage jihad upon at the level of the idea. The solution is to unleash the revelation, the Quran, thereby purging Islamic praxis of the impediments, the structures and worldviews that would deny Islam its duty to now propagate sustainable da'wah in the west in the early 21st century.

THE CASE OF MILITARY ACTION BY MUSLIM MINORITIES.

The attempted coup d'etat of the Jamaat al Muslimeen of Trinidad and Tobago from 27th July 1990 to August 1st 1990 was simply that, an attempted coup d'etat. It was Libyan funds that enabled the purchase, collection and mobilisation of materiel necessary for the military strike. Likewise Libya trained the core commando group in the Libyan Desert that stormed the House of Representatives in session on July 27th 1990 thereby precipitating a hostage crisis, the chosen instrument to effect political change outside the ambit of constitutional instruments.

But the funds or training did not constitute a military strike on the House of Representatives. That Bilaal Abdullah would repeatedly travel to the US with the Libyan funds in his possession; purchase arms and ammunition in various gun shows; purchase, store and package said arms and ammunition in Florida and successfully ship the arms and ammunition to Trinidad and Tobago speaks volumes of either US federal and state governments' incompetence or complicity with the Jamaat al Muslimeen.

The evidence points to complicity for in the period 1989-1990 US Washington elites were involved with various Muslim groups to attain their specific geo-political ends. Why then were covert agencies of the US government willing to consort with the Jamaat al Muslimeen in 1989-1990 to enable this small grouping in Trinbagonian society to launch an attempted coup d'etat in 1990? The best reason so far uncovered is the drive for energy security and the geo-political imperatives of the control of natural gas/LNG.

Is it simply coincidence that by 1992 after the return to political power of the PNM (Peoples National Movement) after being decimated by the NAR (National Alliance for Reconstruction) in 1986 the then PNM government headed by Patrick Manning signed into existence with AMOCO Train 1 of Atlantic LNG? Does the same coincidence reoccur when in December 2001 after a tied general election result of 18-18 between the PNM and the United National Congress (UNC) then in government the decision was taken by the then President of the Republic of Trinidad and Tobago to hand over the reigns of government to the PNM? Was that a coup d'etat by constitutional means?

The common thread to both instances was the geo-political realities of a secure energy supply to the US. On its accession to state power in a coalition with the NAR in its first term negotiations between the UNC and the partners of Atlantic LNG for the creation of Trains 2 and 3 of Atlantic LNG were at times rocky and adversarial in the public domain at best. Although trains 2 and 3 were signed off by the UNC government further expansion of Atlantic LNG were publicly dismissed by UNC functionaries.

The unitisation of cross-border gas reservoirs with Venezuela is a priority for the gas major BP that dominates the Trinbagonian gas sector, but President Chavez of Venezuela signed no Memorandum of Understanding (MOU) with the UNC governments of 1995-2000 and 2000-2001. The said Memorandum of Understanding (MOU) would be signed with the PNM administration in 2003.

The final nail in the UNC coffin was its open, public embrace of al Qaeda sympathisers and operatives in the 2000 and 2001 general elections campaigns whilst it attacked its former ally of the 1991, 1995 and 2000 general elections: the Jamaat al Muslimeen. The message sent to the US Washington elites and the federal covert agencies post September 11th, 2001 was that a UNC government post 9/11 openly consorted with the enemies of the US thereby constituting a clear and present danger to US interests in the Caribbean, The rest is history.

The US thereby empowered the Jamaat al Muslimeen to launch the military strike on the House of Representatives in 1990 to serve the interests of the US. The Muslimeen's action was not defensive, neither was a pre-emptive strike on a hostile NAR government. The alliance between US interests and the Muslimeen meant that Islamic sensibilities were banished from the action taken for there was no way that the leadership of the Muslimeen could have walked away from the alliance and survive to this date.

All attempts to make peace from within the international Ummah were rebuffed because the leadership of the Muslimeen were mesmerized not by the negative effects such action would have on Islam in Trinbago but by the hint, the smell, the expectation of political power and influence. Bilaal Abdullah stands guilty of being more enthralled by the hint of political power in 1990 than Yasin Abu Bakr. The lust for political power drove the leadership of the Muslimeen to dance with the kufr and it was Indian racist hegemony within the Ummah that drove the Muslimeen into the arms of the kufr.

The relentless discourse of the Jamaat al Muslimeen as a terrorist organisation is simply the means for the US Washington elites to clean up the loose ends left in Trinbagonian society after the hostage situation at the House of Representatives was resolved on the 31st July 1990 without the decimation of the Muslimeen hostage takers and the hostages. The efforts to link the leadership of the Muslimeen to international muslim organisations marked as enemies of the US has to be relentless for this is the thin edge of the wedge inserted into the political order of Trinidad and Tobago in 2004.

It is the desire for political power and self-aggrandisement coupled to a worldview heavily influenced by Mawdudi and Qutb that resulted in the deliberate refusal of the Muslimeen to contest in the kufr courts the injunction applied for and granted to the Port of Spain City Corporation in December 1984. This deliberate refusal, this deliberate act which indicated that the Muslimeen chose confrontation, military engagement over legal action allowed an affidavit sworn to by a racist Indian hegemonist who was a Muslim cleric to be untested, to escape scrutiny in a court of kufr law and hence to influence future legal action on the issue of the occupancy of the land at No.1 Mucurapo Road, Port-of-Spain.

The desire of confrontation, for military confrontation with a kufr state by a muslim minority sets in train a dynamic that to date has always worked to the detriment of Islam and the devotion of the muslim organisation to the praxis of Allah (swt). The potent examples of this dynamic are the Jamaat al Muslimeen post 1990 and the muslim engagement with the kufr state in the Philippines.

As a result of the alliances, the actions taken and the complicities involved in the creation and execution of the attempted coup d'etat of 1990, Yasin Abu Bakr and Bilaal Abdullah are today in 2004 politicians still condemned to seek political influence and self-aggrandisement in the kufr political order. Islam in Trinbago has suffered from 1990 to 2004, as the maladies that hobble the da'wah of the Ummah in Trinbago have not disappeared, they have in fact worsened with the addition to the brew of al Qaeda sympathisers and sleeping assets.

Glossary

Allah (swt): The holy and revered name of the One that speaks to human creation in these times through the revelation of the Holy Quran.

Dajjal: 'the cheat' or 'the charlatan'.

Dar ul Harb: The land or abode of war exists where Muslims live under the Hegemony of jahiliyya under the rule of kufr/unbeliever law. A most problematic reality for Muslim minorities of the west as traditional/Islamic jurisprudence doesn't grapple with this reality.

Dar ul Islam: 'The abode of Islam'. The space or geographic entity under the hegemony of Islam.

Da'wa: The propagation of Islam amongst the unbelievers through outreach programs of various means and structures.

Din: The faith that is Islam.

Fatwa: A pronouncement or ruling on any issue affecting the practise of Islam.

Haram: All that is forbidden and unlawful in Islam. All that abrogates Islam.

Holy Quran: Allah (swt) has chosen through the ages to speak to human creation via prophets who announce the revelation of Allah (swt). In this phase of the history of human creation the physical manifestation and evidence of Allah's (swt) revelation is the book the Holy Quran.

Infidel: Kafir. One who rejects Islam and the foundation of Islam, Tawhid.

Islam: the Muslim religion rooted in the revelation of the Quran,

Jahiliyya: The abode, realm or state of existence in rebellion to the will of Allah(swt). This state of rebellion stands in sharp contrast to the state of being in submission to the will of Allah (swt). Islam/jahiliyyah are then dualities locked in persistent contradiction as they relentlessly battle for hegemony and suzerainty over human creation and the earth itself.

Jihad: An all-encompassing concept that defines the relationship of the Muslim to Allah (swt). The submission of the Muslim to the will of Allah (swt) is in fact articulated through jihad or striving in the way of Allah (swt) The Muslim is then called upon to give of his/her very being and all of their talents, wealth, resources to ensure the hegemony of Islam. Each and every Muslim must give of their specific and unique blessings from Allah (swt) to ensure the dominance of Islam, whether it is money, lands, buildings, products of the hand, of the mind, of the land all Muslims must strive in the way of Allah (swt).When the need arises to physically defend Islam, Muslims are then called upon to make the ultimate form of jihad, which is martyrdom.

Kharijite/s: Literally 'those who seceded'. Muslims who insisted that non-Kharijites Muslims were kafirs and must have jihad waged on them.

Kuffir/kufr: An unbeliever by dint of the fact that he/she/they fail to submit to the will of Allah (swt) through non-acceptance of the praxis of Islam. A kufr is then an adherent to the realm of rebellion/jahiliyyah and by extension an enemy of Islam.

Munafikun: Hypocrites. The enemies of Islam within the ambit of Islam.

Muslim: One who submits to the will of Allah as revealed in the Holy Quran.

Purdah: The praxis of the seclusion of Muslim women premised upon male hegemony.

Quran: The Holy Book of Islam.

Salafiyya: Derives from the Arabic word salaf meaning 'ancestors' or 'predecessors' The term is used to refer to (a): the generation of the Ansars of the Prophet Muhammad (uwbp) and those that followed. Shia Islam rejects the praxis of those of this generation/grouping that resented the hegemony of the blood line of the Prophet (uwbp). (b) Those that reject the discourse of Abduh and Al-Afghani use the term in a derogatory manner.

Shahid: The martyr of Islam. The Muslim who dies in the defence of Islam.

Shariah: The Law of Islam.

Ulema: The scholars of Islam.

Ummah: The body of believers, Muslims who in their submission to Allah (swt) constitute a people which cuts across boundaries and limitations created by nationalism, racism, and all other concepts of exclusivity.

References

"Abu, Musab Al-Zarqawi". www.iraqcoalition.org/transcripts/20040212_zarqawi full.html.

Abul-Fadl, Mona 1991: "Beyond Cultural Parodies and Parodizing Cultures. Shaping a Discourse." The American Journal of Islamic Social Sciences Vol. 8; No.1 of 1991.

al Alwani, Taha J. 1991: "Taqlid and Ijtihad." The American Journal of Islamic Social Sciences Vol. 8 No. 1 of 1991.

Al Qaeda Training Manual.

Brown, Dee 1976: "Bury my heart at Wounded Knee". Bantam Books. New York.

Dale, Stephen Frederic 1980: "Islamic Society on the South Asian Frontier The Mapillas of Malabar 1498-1922". Oxford. London.

Damrel, David 1995: "The Religious Roots of Conflict Russia and Chechnya." http://www.iol.ie/~afifi/Articles/chechnya.htm

"Darfur Rising: Sudan's New Crisis". 25th March 2004. International Crisis Group. Africa Report No.76 Nairobi/Brussels.

"Darfur Destroyed Ethnic Cleansing by Government and Militia Forces in Western Sudan". Human Rights Watch May 2004 Vol. 16, No. 6 (A)

Davis, Leonard 1989: "Revolutionary struggles in the Philippines". Macmillan. Hong Kong.

Echo of Islam. No. 109/110 July/August 1993.

Echo of Islam No. 116 February 1994.

Enayat, Hamid 1982: "Modern Islamic Political Thought: the response of the Shi'i and Sunni Muslims to the 20th century." Macmillan Press Ltd. London.

"Facts about Taliban". A Pamphlet. www.afghan-politics.org

fatwa-online.com. www.fatwa-noline.com/muslimminorities/index.htm.

"Fatwa urging jihad against Americans". February 23rd 1998. www.ict.org.il/articles/fatwah.htm.

Finch 3rd Major Raymond C. 1997: "a face of Future Battle: Chechen Fighter Shamil Basayev". www.aeronautics.ru/chechnya/basayev.htm.

Francisco, Luzviminda 1987: "The Philippine-American War" in "The Philippines Reader" edited by Daniel B. Schirmer and Stephen Rosskamm Shalom. South End Press. USA.

Heikal, Mohammed 1981: "Iran; the untold story." Pantheon Books. New York.
"IbnTaymiyyah on Jihad".
www.allaahuakbar.net/scholars/ibn_taymiyyah_on_jihad.htm.

Irfani, Suroosh 1983: "Iran's Islamic Revolution". Zed Books Ltd. London.

Jameelah, Maryam 1980: "The Resurgence of Islam and our liberation from the colonial yoke". Mohammed Yusuf Khan and Sons. Pakistan.

Kettani, M. Ali 1986: "Muslim Minorities in the world today." Mansell Publishing Ltd. London.

Mansur, Salim 1980: "The Political Significance for muslims of the Islamic Revolution in Iran" in Echo of Islam No. 109/110 July/August 1993. University of Western Ontario.

Mawdudi, Sayyed Abul Ala 1994: "The Punishment of the Apostate according to Islamic Law".

Mawdudi, Sayyed Abul Ala 1981: "Towards Understanding Islam." The UK Islamic Mission. London.

May, R.J. 1985: "The Philippines after Marcos". Ed. By R.J. May and Francisco Nemenzo. Croom Helm. London.

"Mujahid Usama Bin Ladin 1996: The New Powder keg in the Middle East". Nida ul Islam. October-November 1996. www.islam.org.au/articles/15/LADW.HTM.

Nasr, Seyyed Hossein 1972: "Sufi Essays". George Allen and Unwin Ltd. London.

Nasr, Seyyed Hossein 1981: "Islamic Life and Thought". George Allen and Unwin Ltd. London

Netton, Ian Richard 1992: "A Popular Dictionary of Islam". Curzon Press. UK.

Noble, Lela Garner 1987: "Muslim Grievances and the Muslim Rebellion". In "Rebuilding a Nation Philippine Challenges and American Policy". Edited and introduced by Carl H. Lande. Washington Institute Press. USA.

Noble, Lela Garner 1987: "The Muslim Insurgency" in "The Philippines Reader" edited by Daniel B. Schirmer and Stephen Rosskamm Shalom. South End Press. USA.

Noori, Ayatollah Allama Yahya 1985: "Islamic government and Revolution in Iran." Royston Ltd. Scotland.

The Observer Newspaper. "Last words of a terrorist". Sunday 30th September 2001.

Phelan, John Leddy 1967: "The Hispanization of the Philippines". University of Wisconsin Press. USA.

"Quran": Translated by Abdullah Yusuf Ali. Dar Al-Kitab Al-Mari, Egypt.

"Quran": Translated by M.H. Shakir 1993. Tahrike Tarsile Quran Inc. New York.

Qutb, Sayyid 1982: "This Religion of Islam." Polygraphic Press. Malaysia.

Rodinson, Maxime 1974: "The Western Image and Western Studies of Islam" in "The Legacy of Islam". Edited by Joseph Schacht with C. Bosworth. Oxford. London.

Shuyab, Fiazuddin 1991: "Muslims under Non-Islamic Law." Torch of Islam September 1991 Trinidad

Taheri, Amir 1987: "The Spirit of Allah, Khomeini and the Islamic Revolution." Hutchinson. London.

www.sistani.org/html/eng/menu/2/books/2/inside/33.htm.

www.sistani.org/html/eng/menu/2/books/2/inside/5.htm.

www.sistani.org/html/eng/menu/2/books/2/inside/6.htm

www.sistani.org/html/eng/menu/2/books/2/inside/7.htm.

About the Author

Daurius Figueira was born on the 5th March 1955 in Port-of-Spain, Trinidad in the West Indies. He is married and is the father of one child.

He received his BA (Hons) and MPhil degrees from the University of the West Indies, St. Augustine Campus in Trinidad where he is currently a candidate for his Phd.

Daurius Figueira is a social researcher in Trinidad and Tobago. His research interests include the Illicit Drug Trade in the Caribbean, racist discourse and black on black racism, Islamic discourse and globalisation and its impact on the economy of Trinidad and Tobago with emphasis on the natural gas/lng sector.

His previous publications include:
Cocaine and the Economy of Crime in Trinidad and Tobago published in 1997.

A Spy in the Houses of Hate: The Ironies and Paradox of Black on Black Racism in Post-Colonial Trinidad and Tobago published in 2000.

Jihad in Trinidad and Tobago July 27th 1990 published in 2002.

Simbhoonath Capildeo, Lion of the Legislative Council and Father of Hindu Nationalism in Trinidad and Tobago published in 2003.

Exiting a Racist Worldview A Journey through Foucault, Said and Marx to Liberation published in 2004.

Index

0-595-33613-2